Poetical Praise Passion and Politicking

By Anthony Dixon

Cover concept by Anthony Dixon
Graphic Designer: Gene F. Brady Jr.

Picture on back: Depiction of Horsehead
and Flame Nebulae in Orion

Poetical Praise, Passion, and Politicking

ISBN

9798374618075

A Message From The Author:

Without a positive revolution, there will not be a peaceful solution to the problems we're facing in every nation. Leading to only more confusion, and a deceased conclusion to what we all know as life;

We are all family, so we need to come together as family;
to embrace the trace of our family tree;
dating back to G.O.D.,
or pay his heavy and heavenly price!

Take no offense to any comments made in this book on race, religion, or just plain reality!

This book is based on the truth, and my own educated guesses.

I don't discriminate, nor am I a racist;
because I will not allow myself to be plagued by this
killer disease known as hatred!

Poetical Praise, Passion, & Politicking
Author: Anthony Dixon

This book is dedicated to
the Great Ones who made this possible!
The Lord, God Almighty; my ancestors,
parents, family, friends, and all of the positive
influences; plus inspirations that have
enlightened my life thus far!

I sincerely Thank You!

Acknowledgements

I would like to pay my respects to my family and friends who helped mold me into the individual that I am today. God bless your soul Grandma; you did a great job at raising me. I only wish that you could see me now! You will always be in my heart! Mable S. Allen, R.I.P.

To my first Cousin Keith; If it wasn't for you I probably would have never been a writer. I wrote my first rap/poem dedicated to you when you passed. I felt so much grief that I had to write my thoughts and feelings down. I just wish it didn't have to turn out this way. You will always be loved and missed, because family is forever! Keith Archer, R.I.P., Cousin Shonda, R.I.P., Uncle Tea, R.I.P., Uncle Lee, R.I.P. and all the other greats that have passed!

Special thanks to my Uncle Tony Allen, for your support!

Dad, thanks for instilling in me the traits of a hard worker! Because earning comes from learning to a good and honest deserver!

Mom, thanks for carrying me through my first 9 months of joy! I am happy and proud to have been your first born, baby boy!

I want to thank everyone for acknowledging my talent, and helping me bring my vision to life!

Content

(Continue)

Content

(Continue)

Content

(Continue)

Content

Capitalization and punctuation are stressed to signify the importance of statements in some lines, and to show a pause between words and lines when being recited.

Introduction

Poetical Praise, Passion, and Politicking is a poetical trilogy composed of three major issues that address life from four different angles.

1. Poetical- Poetry at its' finest!
2. Praise- Enlightening Spiritual Poems
3. Passion- Love Poems inspired by past & present relationships and experiences.
4. Politicking-Revolutionary/Political poems inspired by the struggle.

This literary work emphasizes my thoughts and feelings on God, love, and the worldly matters that we as people face each and every day. Instead of adding to the problems; it is time to find the solutions to the mass confusion, because we are losing precious lives, time, and oxygen from pollution; dating back to an in-equal Constitution; that set off a revolution; not because of evolution, but because revelations continues proving that this nation, under God, indivisible, with liberty and justice for all; will fall if we don't really put all of our differences aside and stand tall; together, forever, to praise our Heavenly Father for our creation. So what are you going to say, and where are you going to go when the Lord calls? I wish you well on your test of Faith!

A Growing Love

I love you more and more everyday,
and I am so very happy to say that we have a knowing love!
Showing love to each other unconditionally
in many different ways!
We have a growing love that will touch the heavens above,
and reflect back down to us intertwined with the suns' rays!
That wraps us up in its' warm blanket of sunshine,
it's fun time, and summertime in the city around lunchtime!
My lady's looking pretty as crisp, fifty dollar bill
as we enjoy our meal she turns on more sex appeal!
It's about time to leave this bar and grill,
because we've already had our fill of food,
now it's time fulfill our thrills, and groove to a smoother
mood!
Slow dancing, then romancing, how enchanting!
She's panting; caught up in one of my love spells that never
fails! Her fingernails slide down my back like hands on
rails!
Leaving marks that start from scratch!
Her eyes are closed; blindly reading me like brail!
I inhale as she exhales!
We're a perfect match, because opposites attract!
We go together!
Where ever it may be;
through any kind of weather,
for worse or for better
we have a growing love forever,
that is watered, and nurtured by each other!

5/5/05

All About: A Growing Love

Usually the longer you know someone; the better you know them, and the better your relationship becomes. I said usually, because there are the exceptions of the people who consider themselves in the category of: The Players! You basically can spot them from a mile away, or tell by the way that they carry themselves.

The most attractive people often fall into this category because they have a larger fan base, but it truly depends on the individual. Some players are hard to detect, but their desires lead them into having more current affair episodes than the television show. It is a dirty game and the players play it for keeps! The truth be told! Faithful relationships have a more positive outcome if you're not adding up the tally of scores like players; who score big thinking it's a plus, and are most of the time big time losers, and negative zeros! Faithfulness displays morals, values, and promising things in life; unlike players who temporarily get satisfaction from their objects of attraction!

With all the killer diseases being passed around; everyones' playing days should be over, but for some it is a favorite pass time leading them to their last time! They are carelessly using excuses like: they only live once, so they're going to have a ball until they fall! That's a risky pass time that I'll pass on anytime! I rather have a growing, knowing, and showing love with the one woman I truly love, and loves me in return faithfully!

Love and by: Anthony Dixon

A Lost Love (Dedicated to Natasha)

A lost love is like a lonesome dove tossed into the air
to roam freely up above without the precaution of a care;
No one knows if it will ever return or not;
You only know that there's a spot in your heart for it
that is yearning and burning hot!
That space can not be replaced,
and cheap thrills aren't able to fill its' slot;
Because it belongs to a lost love
to prove they haven't forgot;
Even though their heart may not forgive,
they will forget me not!
and if I should fail;
It still was at least worth a shot;
I care for my lost love!
I swear, I care a lot;
because she is the only one in the world
that can make my teardrops stop;
For her my love still burns, I just hope she returns,
before my time runs out on the clock!

9/6/05

A New Couples' Love

In the mourning, when we arise with the sunrise,
and are born again with a new day;
To come face to face with the sun,
we just may become one;
How long it lasts, depends on you,
to decide when we separate,
and once again become two;
For example, here's a sample…
Two strangers meet on the streets;
get to know each other for a while,
and end up making each others lives' complete;
Together forever to believe and achieve,
mountain high feats;
From a love that started off shallow,
but became so very deep!

12/18/04

All About: A New Couples' Love:

This poem was a token of my love and appreciation to one of the ex-ladies in my life, the second day after we met. I told her about my past that lead up to the present, and touched on what I desired for my future; a true relationship. It was the introduction to the start of a brand new life for her and myself. A story of how two strangers meet and become one, together with possibilities of forever that I had always longed for. She was in my corner for a good while, and I loved and appreciated her for that. She was the first woman who had ever been with me when I was down and out, without a dime, and without peace of mind. It worked out for a while because we were just like couples should be; there for each other through thick and thin. We had our times with arguments leading up to separation more times than I could keep up with, but she always came back after she cooled off to mend our bond. I was thankful and grateful for her to be my lady, by my side, and in my corner. This is for one of the special ladies that I had given my heart to in life.

Love and by: Anthony Dixon

Anthony Dixon

A Perfect World

A perfect world would be full of
love, peace, and happiness;
without rape, hate, violence, or sadness;
It would be a world of unity,
in each and every community;
without poverty or starvation in any nation;
A world without an overpaid crooked political party,
neither republican or democracy;
A world full of peaceful demonstrators,
without player haters and dictators;
It would be heaven on earth,
without shame and nothing in vain;
people openly making love,
and walking naked in the rain
With women giving birth to generations
that would never die
and our technology would allow us to fly,
and soar more than millions of miles
beyond our own skies,
to populate other perfect worlds;
Life would be one great celebration,
to show our appreciation;
There would be no jealousy, temptation,
or careless actions taken;
because everyone would show,
the utmost respect and consideration;
While meditating and practicing life preservation;
It would be a perfect world,
where creative minds could freely be creative;
a place where no one was foreign,
everyone a native;
We would work together,
to help make each others' lives better;

by growing our own crops,
and cultivating the land;
Every child of ripe age, woman, and man;
With loving arms extending out their
caring and sharing hands;
Everything would be free,
free from disease and free to give and receive;
There wouldn't be any limits,
to what we all could achieve;
but for there to be a perfect world,
we would all have to believe.

5/8/05

All About: A Perfect World

The vision of a perfect world exists in the minds of most people, or maybe even all people. If it was a perfect world in perfect harmony, and everyone had everything that they needed, wanted, and desired; I don't see why everyone wouldn't be happy.

I know that I would! That is the kind of world that I have always wanted to live in! A world of true peace, love, and happiness! We need it, but to receive it we must first have to believe in it.

At least we can act as if it was, and show love, peace, and happiness in our own actions.
We must first start with ourselves, because if we as individuals lived out this vision; our visions would be in sync with the same goal of having a perfect world.

What more could anyone ask for?

Love and by: Anthony Dixon

A Poor Mans' Hope

A poor mans' hope exceeds all others' hope,
fore he has nothing and everything
to hope for at the same time;
Rather than a rich man,
whose needs are met with very large checks,
but his greed only makes him hope
for more and more dollar $igns;
It's a big difference in the significance
of a poor man having zero,
and in the eyes of many being one;
because a rich mans' zeros are added together
to make one large sum;
That's right, they zero in, on denieros,
then, are appreciated like big heroes,
when, the money they burn,
probably wasn't earned,
but wealth stolen by the self chosen,
because for a poor mans' hope,
they are not concerned.

Jan. 2005

All About: A Poor Mans' Hope

Being a poor man myself, and having my ups and downs financially; I can touch on this subject with unwanted bonafide experience. Unwanted: because no one wants to be poor, and bonafide: because when it comes to poverty; I am definitely over qualified for the position. My feelings towards the way the world is when it comes to wealth and power/ poverty and weakness guided me with the insight to write this poem. It is indeed wrong in my eyes and I easily voice my facts about situations with such importance. It's a shame that some people are without jobs, housing, and food in the United States, when it is the wealthiest country in the world.

There is no understanding when it comes to how people can give away zillions of dollars to lucky or crooked individuals in lotteries, and games; but not follow one of the ten commandments from God to comfort thy neighbor. Some of these so called Christians are the most ruthless beings on the earth; robbing the poor blind to get rich. They must be the Anti-Christ using religion as a front to cover up the evil that they take part in. It's a crying shame, and the tears of pain are being shed by the poor everyday!

Love and by: Anthony Dixon

A True Friend

A true friend is something in life
that you should cherish to the end.
I just want to let you know
that ever since I have met you;
that's just what you have been.
A true friend is there for you
whether the situation be thick or thin.
They are someone unforgettable;
not in and out of your life like a trend.
They're there for better or worse,
and it doesn't matter how much money
you have in your purse;
because they are always thinking of your
well being first.
They will quench your dying thirst,
and feed your starving hunger;
whether they've known you short or longer,
because a true friend can even be found in a stranger.
Thank you; all of those who have a good heart
within,
because there is where I know I can find a true friend.

Dedicated to Des and her sister, *from Anthony S. Dixon*
P.S. I wish you much love, peace, and happiness!
God Bless You!

6/17/05

All About: A True Friend

Two of my homegirlz inspired me to write this poem when I was homeless, unemployed, and without a dime in my pocket. On the weekdays I would go to type up my poetry wherever I could but on the weekends I didn't have access to a computer. I couldn't travel too far with my heavy bag of luggage that basically held the only evidence of my identity and dignity. My hardhat, work boots, clothes, and hygiental products added on to the weight of my burdens that I already carried on my shoulder.

One day I stopped at a hot dog stand to get something to eat, and one of the girls told me that her sister said that I was cute. I thanked her for the compliment, and chatted briefly. Every time that I happened to go by on the weekend I spoke to them. One day I was hungry, but my money was a little short so I went and told them my situation and they gave me a break. I thanked them, and it gave me a warm feeling in my heart. Other times came that I was in the same predicament, and they looked out for me, so I told them that I was going to write a poem dedicated to them. After saying that, the name of the poem came to me naturally.

A True Friend: That's what they are; they care, they share, and it comes from their heart. That's exactly what this world needs more of: people looking after the one's they care for and love; like Gods' Angels in the heavens, where the stars shine up above.

Love and by: Anthony Dixon

Abiola

Abiola,
you are beautiful as
the sweet stringed sound of a viola;
Playing a humble note, gently stroked,
and creating a tune as sweet as your perfume
that's enlightening enough to make a rose bloom
like the summer month of June;
Abiola, African Emperess;
Queen of the Mother Land,
showing love to your brotherman;
despite differences on the other hand,
you still understand;
You are wise as the owl,
and mistic as the full moon
that makes the wolves howl;
It is our kingdom to share as a pair,
fore there is no one like us to be found anywhere;
Our crowns are jewels that are rare,
and no one will ever be able to compare;
Truly seen from the eyes of the beholder,
This one is going out to you,
African Emperess, Abiola!

11/4/04

All about: Abiola

This poem was written after I met a beautiful young lady in the New Haven Public Library. Her looks sent me into a trance immediately after laying my eyes on her! The laws of nature propelled me to approach and address what seemed to be this damsel in distress! Her eyes called out, like the call of the wild, as I checked out her style! She was sweet, petite, and looked good enough to eat; but I was already full after indulging myself in her eye candy!

I professed that I was an artist and poet even though the looks of me didn't show it. I guess she admired my mind and personality, because she gave me the time of day; which was my only request. It was just an introduction and chit chat after I was caught into her web of innocent abduction by seduction! I had to at least speak to this beauty of the week, or else live with the regret to only feel cheap!

It was a five minute period that seemed to last a lifetime! She gave me her email address and told me to write her a poem; which I gladly agreed to do. To let her feel the vibe with words of whom she was talking to! This was my chance to mentally romance this woman whose beauty had put me into a trance! I knew that I didn't have a chance with her in any other way, because I was in a tough position at the time; so I took up the offer on writing her; so I could get at and attract her mind!

Never avoid your feelings! Just go with the flow and you will see, as your current connects with the waves of the ocean to mentally set you free!

Love and by: Anthony Dixon

Alone in a War Zone

I'm alone facing the cold like stone!
Which left me stone cold, and young but looking old!
My body is numb from feeling,
and aged by the elements of time
frozen within, leaving my thoughts preserved like wine,
yet still I am standing bold;
While watching how unkind is some human kind,
because they are not warming, but tearing at my soul!
My significant other is the pen that I hold,
while plenty of my thoughts are fought
by many imbalances caught
in the eyes of my intelligence!
started by mistakes made
from someone elses' negligence!
Effecting me like an earthquake,
and giving me the shakes!
The legendary Curtis Blow once said,
(These are the Breaks!)
but I refuse to be broken, unless I'm breaking
after these lines I have spoken,
or breaking taking five for smoking;
unless I'm break dancing,
or breaking it down on the floor,
while having a good time jamming...
or perhaps pressing the brakes,
because there's some man standing
in the middle of the road holding a sign saying;
now's the time! Chanting
kidnap and crash the whole political party
and hold them for ransom!
To- see- just- who - comes to there rescue;
because I know it won't be me,

to free those crooks hiding behind the
red, white, and blue,
but just out of curiosity will it be you?
Volunteering as a new recruit to shoot!
It might even be Osama Bin Laden,
and his Al-Qaida crew!
Coming to get their money,
that they feel is well over due.
Money paid to put up their mirage
to camouflage The World Trade Centers' sabotage!
I can see those pieces coming together,
by the artists of this collage; can you?
As I slave for minimum wage
trying to get a piece of this American Pie;
they track me down for bills I haven't paid,
and keep such a very close eye,
but claim they couldn't track one of those terrorists,
when it was obvious they were spies!
They knew the truth, but covered it with lies!
burned the proof,
now everyday another soldier dies!
Another mother and sister cries,
along with another father and brother
mourning the loss of a family member
in which they had very strong ties!
I don't think Bush even has the courage
to look them in their eyes
from the guilt of his greed to succeed and lead
a whole nation into inflation and filth;
because he rather order someone else,
to take all of his risks!
In fear of being inferior,
he refuses to be on the list of his own death wish!
If you ask me, Bush should be renamed to Douche,
and ordered to rinse his own sour puss

when he goes to cleanse the dirt off his hands
from his oil spoiled plans!
We should im-peach this fuzz
before his appeal kills all of U.S.;
for those that didn't catch the hint, - that's us!
How can we trust a Bush if it isn't the burning bush;
when in God We Supposed To Trust!
What Bush isn't learning
is that one day his bush maybe burning
in hell for mass murder in Operation Shush!
He didn't see any proof of scuds,
or missile intelligence!
He started war just because of greed,
on the strength that he's the president!
Which isn't a good enough excuse,
on top of lacking backing evidence!
Now they're probably tapping
every phone in the world wide residence,
and listening to your private conversations
claiming they're trying to track terrorists!
This capital Wuss Bush
is a manipulative master mind of slavery,
using any countries' soldiers' bravery
to take his own chances.
So now, every day and every night,
with death! Another soldier dances!
They knocked down,
The World Trade Center to the ground
for attention and left it the Center of Attention!
The C.O.A. leaving so many D.O.A.
I wish that Christ or Allah
had intervened in prevention of this Jihad;
that left so many peoples' lives and cries in suspension
from the impact and collapse
of those airplanes descension!

I know just how something so terrible
was allowed to happen;
because Negligent President Bush is in office,
and not Jesse Jackson!
An excuse is not needed!
What is needed is action!
It has long past the point of perfect timing
for a change to come, securing civil satisfaction!
I am not asking any questions
of those showing aggression,
because too many so called leaders are lying, and stealing;
misleading in the wrong direction!
I rather read from top breed resources
to check the correct spelling!
Then apply the mind of my own
for a wise interpretation,
so, who are you telling?
Those that made change for minimum wage
back in the days are now retiring,
and social security is failing!
When it should and must be tightened,
because if not! The effects will be frightening,
and striking like lightning!
Leaving more than just the retired and elderly ailing!
Gas prices are steadily climbing,
and inner-cities crimes rising!
Which is not surprising, if you look at the figure books
of the crooks that are Wall Street scaling!
Bad money handling, or high class gambling
like world class poker; where stock broker jokers,
are getting richer and the poor are still scrambling!
While they're lamping in the Hamptons' and camping,
we're trying to get section- eight public housing, and
more understanding about our closest peers' vanishings!
By demanding explanations like why are disgraced,

drug selling, illegal possession with a weapon felons,
allowed to take promising, scholastic grades excelling -
brothers and sisters lives
off the face of the earth into the dirt, -
when they should be doing time jailing;
The system has long been failing!
Causing people to sing one sad song after another
while screaming and yelling,
because bul-lets are taking the lives of good kids!
When no one knows their destiny from birth
will turn out to be the worst!
Leaving behind family and friends,' feelings hurt!
Mama's crying, because her baby boy's lying in a hearse!
This is more than just a verse!
This is deliverance of a first hand experience,
so take heed and experiment,
with a worth equivalent of JUST-ICE,
because we must discuss this!
We have the freedom of speech, and no one can hush this!
We have to reach to teach and make it public
that our rights are to be stood up for and never to forfeit!
So hold your head up high and say I will never quit!
Standing up for a cause, - not only for one, but for all,
because we as the people have the power,
to change, and create a better aim for these laws
that leave so many apalled, because they are inequal,
and lethal like an injection of oppression!
Creating the mental - part two of slaveries' sequal!
That is taking place today, right now as I speak,
leading the youth astray, thinking they are bad and strong
when they are actually weak! In the mental sense;
because the immense lack of education
has left devastation by knowledge deprivation!
Leaving many African teens to only dream
of a college spring break vacation!

It is time to face the nation,
protest and demand reperations
for our own families kidnapping and seperation!
Many Jews recieved dues for being encaged in concentration camps from Germany, so sweet land of liberty,
where is our compensation?
For my African ancestors being enslaved on plantations?;
Millions of my people were also murdered and slain,
but they took a lot more from my people;
even their homeland and their name!
They stripped their dignity and replaced it with chains,
stole their freedom, raped their women,
hung their men, and laughed as they watched them hang!
And even after they were dead
afflicted their soul with more pain;
until the very last drop of blood,
shed out of their veins!
To flood the ground like mud
leaving uncleanable stains;
as they were drug to the scrubs,
and thrown into the flames!
Why was this the way someone had to die?;
To live once and die a thousand deaths
not even able to cry!
So why should I hold my breath,
or bite my tongue when I breathe for them!
The free breath of life with rights,
which was their only whim;
when I've cried over the thought of all of those lost lives,
sighed and wept!
Feeling like my ancestors are walking with me ,
through the struggle every step by step!
Revealing deep, dark secrets
of what the killers and witnesses minds still kept!
And since then, they have been

restless souls that haven't slept;
that will never forgive and never forget!
So even though we were all born and will die alone;
We should all stand tall and fight,
and if we should fall, then fall together!
then at least we'd know that we stood for freedom forever,
and that we weren't alone in the war zone!

3/6/05

All About: Alone in the War Zone

I wrote this poem to reflect my feelings poetically on my own universal scale of important issues to address. Crooked politicians; a war for the wrong reasons; black on black violence; the caucasion race and their reign of forceful superiority; social security; The World Trade Centers' collapse and the pieces that just don't add up; the homeless; poor; and humanity through the looking glass of my eyes. It's not hard to tell! You name it; it's here. It is the naked truth, and what an ugly sight to behold as the wealthy, healthy, selfishly, rich and powerful try to cover up this scandalous, out of shape whore, called the United States; as it continuously gets raped by Uncle Sam and his bloodthirsty foot soldiers as they terrorize the countries' sides shouting about pride.

I don't see any pride in letting the enemy attack first and then storming their shore. They must have gotten caught with their pants down, raping that whore!(The U.S.) I don't see any pride in raising taxes! I see hungry children dying of malnutrition by the masses, and on top of that sadness; not being taught well enough in their classes! I don't see any pride in making excuses! I see pride in the political party getting kicked in their cabooses! I see pride in a fight to the end without truces! When the real winners, win and the real loser, loses! I see pride, in when the cheaters are disqualified; which only leaves room for the winners to come home with their honor and pride.

To me; it is not all for one and one for all; It is only one for one, because I am the only one on my side! Alone in a War Zone! Until we unite and fight for what is right!

Love and by: Anthony Dixon

Alone

You left me, or should I say unbreathed me!
The last time that my kindness will be mistaken
for weakness!
I used to feel rich in heart,
but you made me feel the cheapest
by keeping all kinds of secrets!
Though I blame myself for having feelings,
because I should have been more careful with
whom I was dealing
before falling for the appealing!
Not knowingly, I wore my heart on my sleeve
only to be deceived,
because I thought you were someone that I could
believe!
With you I only wanted to achieve,
but I guess you were driven by greed!
Only if I knew then,
because now for you my heart bleeds!
I was too late to realize
that I should have been more focused on my needs!
So now, I'm left behind to patch the wounds
that you so deeply imbedded in me; alone!

2004

All About: Alone

This poem is about all of my ex-girlfriends whom I gave my heart and soul to, and they trampled on it like a herd of wild elephants! I found out the hard way that being a gentleman isn't cracked up to what it seems to be, because some females take advantage of whatever they can; however they can! It took me a while to get over the fact that I was a great man who deserved great things, but bad things always came my way! I was a hard working, well paid, well built, and defined brother; who was looking for a real queen to sit on the throne with. I was looking for a real love and found a real fake! A mistake that led to my heartbreak! I didn't know until it was too late that they were no good, in the hood, want to be playa's; that didn't know how to step up to the plate and be real women when a good man came their way. They told nothing but lies and showed deceit that eventually added up and got them caught up, but I still accepted their lame apologies; being the good man that I was. I thought that they would open their eyes to see that I was a good man also, but they were blinded by the glitters and glamour of life that they had only seen and didn't have.

After each break-up; I guess they finally came to their senses, and realized that I was one in a million. They had blown the chance of a lifetime to be with a good man. One ex eventually called me to say that she missed and still loved me. I guess when she left me; another good man was hard to find that she could take advantage of. She probably received the same treatment from them that she had dished out to me, and felt what it really feels like to be played!
Well, all I can say is; to all the real women out there! There are real men also, and I hope that we all meet someone as real as ourselves one day! Peace.

Love and by: Anthony Dixon

Alright

It's going to be alright!
Because I can't allow my worries to turn into fright!
It's going to be alright!
That's what I tell my crazy, southern bell lady night after night!
It's going to be alright!
A better day will soon be in our sight!
Because I am going to do and pursue
everything to make our dreams come true;
to show to you how much that I really do love you,
and that everything is going to be alright!
So don't worry, because I'm going to hurry
to bring complete happiness into our life!

5/11/05

All About: Alright

I thought of this poem one day after telling one of my ex-girls that everything was going to be alright. We were standing outside going through the struggle together when I told her, and I meant every word that I said! I knew there would be a day when cloudy skies and teary eyes were behind us. I didn't know what the future held. I just knew that we were holding each other! No one knows what the future holds. We can only strive, pray, and hope for the best. Nothing is guaranteed in life, but uncertainty!

As long as I'm happy and satisfied with myself that's all that counts! I don't depend on someone else to satisfy me, and make me happy; although I do enjoy positive, passionate company. Their satisfaction is not guaranteed, but self satisfaction and happiness lasts a lifetime! We are all individually responsible for our own feelings and emotions. We must control them, or else they will control us!

Just sit back, relax, and know that everything is going to be alright!

"So don't worry, about a thing! Cause every little thing's, going to be alright!" Bob Marley salute

Love and by: Anthony Dixon

Another Day

Another day!
Weary, dreary,
my eyes are teary,
and longing to be cheery!
Dearly my thoughts are composed,
like the elements of a rose!
Nearly sweet as chocolate to eat,
and like a stream of water they flow!
Seeping through the earth to the root
allowing them to grow,
and bloom to see another day!

2004

All About: Another Day

Under the weather feelings inspired me to write this poem. The traces of my depression fought back by my ways of expression to enjoy, and make the best of even a dull moment. I was going through hard times, and every day to me seemed less of something to look forward to. At the same time I knew that I possessed something great within myself. Something great that external forces would not be able to discourage and destroy! The cries of my unhappiness were longing for cheer, and change to a better position in life! The greatness within myself was striving to complete my tangible goals, and victoriously overcome all obstacles!

The desire that I have to live and never die kept me moving forward, because every day of unhappy times seems like a near death experience! My need to live, learn, and love gave me the drive to push on forward towards tomorrow that I will try to make brighter each day; as I pray and hope to see another tomorrow that will hopefully hold my happiness!

Love and by: Anthony Dixon

Anthony Dixon

Attraction

Deserving is she whom inspires me
to royalty, loyalty, and honesty!
Morgan, I want to thank you for caring,
and sharing your lovely time with me that morning!
I only wish that I had a beautiful bouquet of flowers
that came after Aprils' showers
assorting in a rainbow of colors
to give you that early morning hour!
You are by far one of the prettiest women
that I have ever encountered!
Which is the reason that I showed you two of my poems;
Beautiful along with Desire!
Your persona held a positive karma
like a Madonna filled with love!
Something special that caught my eye
that I take very good notice of!
I had to meet and greet you!
I knew, plus I just had a clue that it would be worthwhile!
I could see the hints of your intelligence
through and beyond your brilliant smile!

You were attractive!
Wait! Let me rephrase that!
Take it back and make it retroactive!
You were so very attractive my temperature started rising,
because you looked hot as volcanic magma!
My heart instantly stopped,
and you jump started it back
with your magic touch that I felt
as it began to melt like plastic!
I felt like the opposite side of a magnet
controlled by the sources of forces in nature
far more greater that the space in between us!

Over powering cowering lust!
That was no match,
as I was being pulled into your magnetic field!
I could not yield, stop, and I did not want to until;
I met you face to face to admire your grace
so I could embrace the moment, but still;
time and place was an opponent
designed in breaking up our component!
As outside forces pulled us apart
physically, but not from the heart!
Causing a brief relief short lasting as a wave crashing,
and splashing upon a tropical coral reef!
Giving me the temporary satisfaction
of your dashing attraction!

Inspired: 11/4/04
3/30/05

All About: Attraction

This poem was at first a formal/poetic email to a lovely lady, whom I met on the bus one morning on my way downtown. The email never went through, but I made a copy of what I had typed out just in case it didn't reach her. I took the precaution, because I had learned from my previous mistakes of my emails not going through properly to be received.

This woman was absolutely beautiful! I didn't even want to take my eyes off of her, because she was so gorgeous! On top of that she was the most pleasant woman in my eyesight at the time being. I wish that I saw her more often, because she made my attention span broaden! She looked like a Yale student dressed so colorful, and carried herself as if brilliant without even having to say a word.

That's powerful! I was reading all of this energy just from her appearance. Somewhat premeditated; I happened to have my poems with me, and I knew just which ones to bring to her attention. I introduced myself after I asked her if she attended Yale. She replied, "yes, and how did I know?"

I told her that she just stands out like a rose amongst weeds, as I gave her two of my favorite poems to read: Beautiful and Desire; which I knew would set her heart on fire! She wanted to keep them, but I couldn't let her because they were the only copies of them that I had at the time.

The ride was short, but very much appreciated when she took the time to read and compliment me on my poems. I thanked her as she passed me her email address before she walked off the bus, and out of my life; possibly for forever!

Love and by: Anthony Dixon

Back Against the Wind

My back is against the wind;
blowing me away from family and friends;
now only the wind has my back
to push me through thick and thin;
I don't even bother anymore to take steps;
I just lift my feet and there in the air they are swept;
kept like the deepest, darkest secrets
that you've only dreamed of when you slept;
but the wind keeps me moving forward
on a straight and narrow path;
It helps me when I am tired, and almost expired
when I can not walk the distance fast;
It gives me encouragement,
to continue my daily task;

and it cools me off when I am hot on the spot
with a smooth refreshing blast!
So my back is against the wind,
and I am going with the grain,
because it carries me where I need to be,
across the sea, and beyond the grassy plains.

4/22/05

Beautiful

Amazingly, I can see you from afar,
and say yes you are more beautiful than a twinkling star!
But for such of a sight to behold;
comparison is embarrassing;
Fore your beauty alone touches the soul!
There is none equivalent to your stunning appearance,
or is as tasteful as you with your graceful deliverance!
Even your skin complexion is toned to perfection!
Any man would be out of their mind
if they ever thought towards you with rejection!
When even the finest of compliments
would not make any sense!
To such of a sight as yourself
they'll be lucky to get a glimpse,
or better yet, a touch of such beauty to behold;
because out of all Gods' creations you are more beautiful!

12/22/03

All About: Beautiful

I was inspired to write this poem, and seven others by a beautiful woman that I had secretly fallen deeply in love with; just by physical attraction. I thought to myself that we would make a perfect couple, because we were around the same size and height; her birthday was day before mines, and also on my grandmothers' memorial day. Last, but not least her beauty was in a category of its' own! Wow! I flipped head over heels for this mystery lady! She was still like a complete stranger to me, but at the same time I felt a connection that was nothing like I had ever felt in my life!

She puzzled me, but I remained to be a complete gentleman because I didn't want to come on to her too strong. I was patiently hoping that she would feel the same thing that I was feeling, but it never happened! She told me that, "she thinks that I am an adorable person," and that "I would find a nice lady for myself one day," making it clear that it wasn't going to be her! I left out the fact that she was twice my age, but hey; age is just a number! Once an adult; always an adult, because age doesn't guarantee maturity!

Eventually, I had to finally give up on this dream girl of mines. I did at least manage to take her out for breakfast one morning, and had dinner with her one evening. My financial status had picked up, and I saw her downtown so I asked her did she want to grab a bite to eat. She replied, "yes" and we found a vegetarian spot to have breakfast.

She didn't eat meat, and I didn't mind because spending time with a beauty like her may only happen once in a lifetime! She barely gave me any conversation, but her presence was satisfying enough for me. It was worth a shot, and that's what I gave! I just wish that I wouldn't have missed at capturing her heart!

Only if she knew that she was the lovely lady of my

past dreams and desires. I was mesmerized by the beauty of this cutie that truly set my feelings free. I had visions of her while I was typing this poem to help guide me through the tunnels of love that I was venturing. It is definitely one of my greatest love poems, but I don't personally judge them (compare), because I thought of and wrote them all. They are all considered pieces of myself, but each in a personal frame. I have passed this poem out to many beautiful ladies, whom I felt deserved a poem that was actually written for them.

The bold and the beautiful women of these times with extraordinary shapes and features that make me say; yes Lord! If you undress them with your eyes, maybe you too will see that this is actually paradise and heaven on earth. The ones who haven't realized this yet, are probably to wound up in their imaginations of playing cops and robbers and think that life has to have a tragic ending. We all need to get on the same pages of love, peace, and happiness; and see what beautiful things happen next!

Love and by: Anthony Dixon

Below Freezing

It's below freezing, I'm sneezing,
yet, I'm thrown outside at 7:30 in the morning,
this cold winter season;
This is treason;
Uncle Sams' hush slaves,
are being paid to downgrade;
the value of another persons life,
whether young or old age;
for the simple reason that-,
rich white folks are in control,

and your poor soul's black;
They will give you minimum wage,
but not the chinchillas off of their back;
even in below freezing weather,
when they have coats of fur and leather;
at home that they don't even wear,
hanging on their rack,
because they don't even care;
and many act as if they're satisfied with that;
when their own living conditions,
aren't even fair;
What they should do is petition,
but keep silent because they're scared,
to lose their position and be the next edition,
in the homeless shelters' bed listing;
without a pot to piss in;
probably the same place they worked at,
because sleeping and working there too,
isn't allowed in the contract.

Jan. 2005

All About: Below Freezing

I felt the need to write this poem on a cold winter day of thirty degrees after being told to leave a shelter at seven-thirty in the morning. I had no place to go, but outside along with the many others who were in the same predicament. The shelters' staff said, "that they only allowed in-house-stay-ins for clients inside of the shelter when the weather was life threatening;" which meant to them, "temperatures in the teens, or below zero wind chill factors." I'm pretty sure that if they were also standing outside in thirty degree weather they would agree that it was life threatening! Even though the ones who gave us the boot out, were just doing their job; soldiers following the generals' orders; it doesn't justify the inhumanity of the orders and actions that were taken! Right is always right, and wrong is always wrong! That's the bottom line!

This long chain of command falls from the almost untouchable politicians who sets the laws, and gives the orders to the touched communities of our society that have-to deal with the corruption and effects of greedy politics. They are crippling the able; trying to make us unstable citizens of society! There should be places to go, things to do, and good people that care enough to help these people in these situations; instead of kicking them while they are down! It's a shame and the wealthy, lawless, crooks are to blame!

Love and by: Anthony Dixon

Boy Toy (9/6/05)

I understand that you have a man,
and that I wasn't in your plans.
But just let me be your boy toy
to give you your rightful amount of joy!
What we had; we don't have to destroy,
or make it obvious by holding hands!
Just let me be your boy toy when you are hot,
so I can cool you off like a fan!
Stay with me, play with me,
and do as you please!
I'm all yours to explore, and I'm pretty damn sure
that anyone quite like myself ever came with such ease!
Just let me be your boy toy to tease, pretty please!
No matter whether I'm up, down,
or on my hands and knees!

Burned Bridges

Bridges crossed, bridges burned;
money spent, money earned;
asked questions, answers learned;
many numbers waiting turns;
All in line at the same time,
with the same thing in mind;
The root to all evil,
because a good thing was hard to find;
In a world where love is blind,
and filled with hate and crime;
I'm still trying to cross these ridges,
almost tripping, while pulling up my britches;
because I dropped my belt,
in one of those deep dug ditches;
while I was passing over,
but I'll go back and get it,
when I'm crossing backover my unburned bridges.

10/6/04

All About: Burned Bridges

I wrote this poem in reference to the relativity of all the people in this world with aspirations of living the reality of the good life. Buying the best foods, cars, and the best of everything else that money can buy.

The key word money; which many people refer to as the root of all evil is also what everyone needs, and are after in this world to survive. People go about many different-ways of getting money. Some right and some wrong. Those right; earn it honestly, and those wrong; get it by any means that they can! Regardless of the people they may hurt, or the consequences that lie ahead. Some people use other people for whatever they can, and then when they can return the favor; they don't! They sure have some kind of nerve! That's what I call, burning bridges! Not showing loyalty by not returning the favor back to those who lent it first! That's one of the most selfish and backstabbing things a person could do! Some people even burn bridges, and then go back to the same person to ask them for another favor. Unless it is a family member, I guarantee that the answer won't be same! They have lost out on what was a bond between two people willing to give each other a helping hand, until one of them decided to be deceiving!

Who knows when they might need someone elses' helping hand? So I wouldn't burn down any bridges if I were you! You'll never know when you might need to cross that bridge in the future!

Love and by: Anthony Dixon

By My Side

Stay there, please care, and keep me company!
By you being by my side;
do you realize what you've done to me?
You've allowed me to love again; companion and friend!
Through good times, and bad times; please stay to the end!
Comfort me when I need to be,
and I will do the same unto thee!
If you could, I wish you would;
be there for eternity!

2004

All About: By My Side

I wrote this poem along with several others with the intentions of winning one womans' heart. This woman was beautiful in everyway, and I desired to be with her dearly. I wrote her passionate poems hoping that she would be in-return compassionate, and not throw them away. We chit chatted in brief conversations that ended quickly due to her not wanting to pay me any attention. I told her the truth with every line, but I guess she failed to believe every word that I said, even though I desirably wanted to make her mines!

Through my eyes we looked like a perfect couple, but she said that, "I wasn't her type." I approached her like a gentleman, but I only came close enough to write! She put up a defense mechanism similar to a concrete wall, enclosing herself in. I tried to penetrate those walls with words hoping that they would either fall, or that she would open her heart to let me in!

Up to that point the only reception I had received from her was rejection, but the longer that we were in each others presence and the more time that passed by; I started to see a change in her attitude towards me. I started to notice glances at me from her direction, and a different look into her eyes. She finally admitted that I was a sweet heart and an adorable person, but she still said that I wasn't her type. She made me think that it was because she was twice my age; which makes reality bite!

She looked as if she had drank from the fountain of youth; preserving her beauty. She looked like she was in her mid-twenties, but her silver streaked, wavy, salt and pepper hair gave her true age of around forty away. I thought about the facts that we were both adults and mature; so in this case I felt that age was just a number, and our love still should've endured!

Love and by: Anthony Dixon

Capture The Essence

Before it is too late,
and the beauty of life runs out of your presence;
You must think fast and react quickly,
to capture its' essence!
That just might be the only chance that you get;
to take advantage of this opportunity,
and not have to live with regrets!
By missing out on an essence
that is impossible to forget!
So capture, and get caught into the rapture
like a back-catcher for the New York Mets!
Get a grip! Don't slip!
Even though the surface may be wet!
Don't trip! Tie your shoes,

because we aren't there yet!
Bring plenty of water,
because you're going to work up a sweat!
Capturing the essence isn't easy;
it takes quite some time to get!
But first, you must think fast and react quickly
to be in its' presence;
Because if you are not there,
Then how will you ever capture the essence?

April 2005

All About: Capture the Essence

I wrote this poem to put more emphasis on seizing the moment, and opportunity while the time is still right. Don't let your dreams walk out of the door on you, and pass you by when you have the chance to capture the essence while it is right in front of you! I have failed to capture many essences of opportunity that left me with the regrets of: what if I had stepped up to the plate, and took a shot at the chance of a lifetime? What would have happened? Who knows, until you take that risk of finding out! Instead, my insecurities left me hanging; which made me feel like the chance of a lifetime would do the same!

You never will know until you try, and if you never try then you will never know! Keep your hopes and dreams alive, or suffer agonizing torment! The pain lasts a lifetime because of the stress and heartache of being lonely, and without something that you longed for so long! Seize every beneficiary opportunity that comes your way, and enjoy the unlimited possibilities that they may hold! Capture the essence and watch the doors open and your opportunities unfold!

Love and by: Anthony Dixon

Castles In My Mind

My thoughts are my fortress,
therefore you can not harm this!
My words are my hooks;
my voiceis my lifeline,
and my soul's my harness!
So if you ever break and penetrate
one of my great thoughts;
I'll escape through my secret gates
to one of my many castles;
I will never be caught!
As you try and you fail
this lesson you will be taught!
I am king of my castle!
I've won all of my battles,
and not once have I fought!
My treasure of wisdom,
must be what you have sought;
but it can not be taken!
Neither can it be bought!
I will always be rich,
because I am rich in heart;
and my treasure will leave with me
from this world when I depart!
So until the meantime,
I'm going to sit on the thrones,
of the castles in my mind.

Jan. 2005

All About: Castles In My Mind

I wrote this poem to tell how I will not let negativity and hatred stop me from doing positive things! I will continue to strive, and educate myself regardless of how much the enemy stands in my way! Jealousy brews in the minds of fools who rather hate, and try to take something from someone else; instead of trying to earn it themselves!

My mind is my crown jewel, and it is more valuable to me than any precious stone in the world! Without it, I would not be able to exist! It is my centerpiece, and control center in which I think and organize my beautiful thoughts of bliss. I have one mind, but many castles are inside of it allowing me to weigh my options. I can avoid the traps that other minds set by protecting, and nurturing my own.

Wisdom gained by the mind can never be stolen. It is imbedded deep beneath the surface, and it is not able to be dug up by any outside force. It is internal and not able to be seen, unless in a vision. It is not able to be heard, unless verbally given. I am the king of my mind; which possesses many castles. They are all my homes where I am the ruler of all the thrones!

Love and by: Anthony Dixon

Compassion for My Soul

Without me even asking;
you show me compassion that's everlasting;
The all seeing and knowing
you're showing and telling
all things that are happening!
Whether near, or far away from here,
or there, you are still aware,
and care with a love so rare;
It couldn't be found
within the deepest depths of the ground,
or seen around
all of the city streets
where the people barely sleep!
Anti-socially rarely speak, or make a sound!
The reason being: their stomachs growl,
because they hardly ever eat
in these poverty strictened towns
that need compassion shown to those souls that holc
onto nothing tighter than a dollar and a dream
making them holler and scream
if they fail to reach their dreams and goals!
It seems hard to fight the devils' temptation
of selling your soul for a medal of gold,
but behold the Kings of Kings
as he restores faith
by showing me compassion for my soul!

3/20/06

Congraduations

Many years we've waited and anticipated,
for the day that we would finally be graduated;
From elementary school to middle school,
and from high school to college;
to the working class to come,
where we'll display our knowledge;
As engineers, teachers, lawyers, and doctors;
or professionals in such sports,
as basketball and soccer;
We'll see many things come true,
if we believe in our dreams;
because the harder we work to succeed,
the less harder it'll seem;
We must always remember and never forget;
that only practice makes,
and is the key to what it takes to perfect;
In the end we will all see,
that it was more than well worth it,
when we are rewarded for our practice,
because we deserved it;
Because we can only get out what we put in;
so if we put in one-hundred percent,
then we are sure to win. Congraduations!

2006

All About: Congraduations

I wrote this poem after I was asked to be the graduate speaker at a youth program graduation. It is word-by-word truth, and encouragement blueprinting the foundation of the way to rise up the ladder of success! Believing in yourself is the key to achieving great feats in life. Your life is the ignition, and practice will keep your skilled engine going to make more and better progress!

Graduation was the original name for this poem until I thought it out, and added more life and creativity to it. People congratulate when someone graduates. So I mixed the two together, and the name congraduations became my new way of celebrating graduations.

Love and by: Anthony Dixon

Continue to Help Me Get Through

When my life was on the line,
you were right there in the nick of time!
When people were cruel to me,
Lord, you were always kind!
When I was lost to others,
I was easy for you to find!
When I was over looked because of stereotypical covers,
you saw me, and never acted blind!
When I was in times of darkness,
you allowed your light to shine!
When my times were the hardest,
you showed me an easier stairway to climb!
When my world was in a bind,

you assured my safety, and that everything was fine!
So Lord, it is true when I say that I only have faith in you,
because all my life you've continued to help me get
through!

3/20/06

Crazy and Beautiful!

(A Wild Combination!)

My lady's crazy and beautiful!
(What a wild combination!)
Sometimes she's lazy,
and other times she's so movable.
She can be stimulating,
but also be irritating,
then out of the blue,
so soothing and suitable.
When she relaxes my mind
like the finest bottle of wine;
as she massages my back,
and taps my spine;
in the same way as a masseuse would do.
She's my old lady,
though, I know she maybe knew to you;
So, sometimes I don't mind
her wild and crazy ways,
because I look past and beyond the surface
of the fact that she's black and that she's beautiful.
Baby, you so crazy, but you're my one and only lady;
making the bond that I have with you like crazy glue.
I love to caress and undress you.
You're so sensual and so sexual;

plus your also a complex individual.
The friction of our mixing,
and the ticking of our hearts
might go off in flames and sparks,
because, baby you're the bomb; that's digital!

5/18/05

All About: Crazy and Beautiful
(What A Wild Combination)

One of my crazy and beautiful ex-ladies inspired me to write this poem. I couldn't help but jot down foot notes of her characteristics in detail, because of her crazy ways. Sometimes she could make me as mad as a raging bull, and other times she kept me calm as a windless spring day. She, like some others had two sides to her that truly only someone with my patience could understand, and put up with!

She was gentle as a kitten, but it didn't take much for her to become as fierce as an African lioness defending her cubs! We went through our ups and downs, and probably separated at least fifteen times, but we always managed to get back together. I was happy that we could work out our differences and still be together, but believe me when I tell you that it was a bumpy road that we worked at smoothing out!

My lady's crazy and beautiful, what a wild combination; I thought as I was looking into her cute, brown eyes. Those two characteristics could mean either one of three things: she's either a lot of excitement, a lot of drama, or in my case a lot of both! If you aren't up for it, I suggest that you don't get involved with someone of this nature, or you might live to regret it! Don't forget it! Love can hurt alot!

Love and by: Anthony Dixon

Cursed

I must be cursed,
because my life just keeps getting worse;
and worsens,
leaving me preparing for the worst!
Before I know it,
I'll probably be dying,
lying in a hearse!
Crying from my grave,
not able to rest in peace,
ancestor of the slaves!
Whom lived without happiness,
and died in heartache and pain!
My blood boiled from angers' heat,
pumping through my veins!
I lived to gain,
but it was taken in vain!
The anguish left me,
on the verge of going insane!
So trust me when I say that it hurts,
and my life just can't get any worse;
because it already is,
I must be cursed!

2004

All About: Cursed

I'm not superstitious, but I've had my large share of unfortunate happenings in my life. Experiencing more downs than ups, and getting up after being knocked down; to only get knocked back down again! I wish that I was getting paid to fight this heavyweight, unpredictable bout with lifes' struggles, but I only come out after every round with more scrapes and bruises! This is a fight that I can not afford to lose though, because my life is on the line! No matter how tired I am, I must continue on with victory on my mind.

For so long, I was taking and rolling with the punches that life threw at me, but life must have hit me with a quick lefty and left me dazed and confused! Before throwing in the towel, I finally came back to; fighting back, and giving life my best shots! This is the greatest battle of all times, and I've been getting pounded by the cheap shots of life for too long! I must stop this monotonous chain of bad events that seems more like a black rain cloud, and curse that is following me everywhere that I go!

This poem is about my constant struggle and disappointment of feeling like I didn't get what I was worth, or deserved in life. It tells how my matters got even worse after I thought it wasn't possible. Then when I tried my hardest to succeed, I still failed! Failed my purpose and failed myself! I'm also talking about the domino effects of slavery and oppression that led up to this point and time where it seems like I am cursed by the bad fortune of hatred that is rubbing off in my direction. I try to shake this devil off and look on the bright side of things, but it seems like dark, bad-luck clouds always follow.

Hopefully, one day this feeling will cease; bringing forth a great peace of mind allowing me to cool down, take my time, and recline. Bad consequences come from bad actions, so if you act good then everything should be all good!

Love and by: Anthony Dixon

Dear Gina
(Dedicational poem)

Dear Gina,
It has been a while since I've last seen ya, (you)
but I want you to know that you're the best thing that ever
happened to this dreamer!
I can't wait until the day
that I can put a wedding ring on your finger!
Then we'll romance, and dance to the tunes
of a band and their singer!
I don't need to imagine,
because I know it is going to happen!
You are my dream come true,
and you make me move into action!
You give me pure satisfaction,
and always keep me laughing!
I'm so glad I have the best woman in the world!
I don't care if I'm bragging!
You're so divine that you define the phrase of a good
lover, and I'm so glad that our son Jack has an outstanding
mother!
Tonight when he goes to bed,
and you tuck him under the covers,
tell him to sleep tight, and that Daddy says he loves ya!
Don't worry, because we'll be seeing each other soon;
to treat every second like it was our first honeymoon!
You two are the only ones in my heart
that can fill up my special room.
It is only for you, where my love is true!
I can't wait till I'll be seeing you real soon!

6/10/05

All About: Dear Gina

The word went around fast that I did poetry, and a guy asked me to write a poem for his girlfriend. I told him that I would, and I even assured that his satisfaction was guaranteed. I told him to ask someone else about the poem that I had written for their girlfriend called, Don't Worry. This is another dedicational poem that I poured my mind, body, heart, and soul into.

I strive to achieve fulfillment for not only myself, but for all of my readers, and customers. You'll never read any works of mines that I haven't put astonishing thought, and care into. I must impress my own self with my own words, and I'm a very tough audience member; so remember the pen and notebooks' page is the setting for my stage, and in my performance, I will never surrender!

Love and by: Anthony Dixon

Desire (2004)

My desire burns for you like wild fires!
The flames are unable to be contained!
causing the ashes of love
to be the only remains;
left in this internal inferno!
My breath is the wind,
strengthening the force
behind my soul, eternal!
Causing more fires to begin;
spreading fast through passions' wilderness
destroying all of hates' bitterness;
So new life and new love will grow,
and continue to flourish;
nourished by natures' flow!

All About: Desire

This is another beautiful poem that was inspired by a lovely woman that I spoke of previously. The mystic lady who captured my heart, and held it for hostage without a ransom!

I sat and had a vision of her lovely face in front of mines, as I poured my heart out onto the paper. With love flowing like lava from a volcano; I wrote about the strong, and passionate way that I felt for her.

The power of love is sometimes so overwhelming that nothing can stop it from continuing on. It thirsts for survival feeding off of any attention it can receive from its' object of desire. Feed the fire, and watch as it quickly rises higher! She was the supplier of fuel that I needed to engulf the paper like a blazing inferno! Her hot to trot savvy sent sparks flying through my eyes, and triggered explosions of fireworks going off in my brain! No one in the world could extinguish this burning desire that I felt for her!

All of the water in the ocean could not put out this flame! It burned hotter than the core of the earth, and every sun put together in the center of the universe! Take it from me, and a lesson learned! I suggest that you don't play with desires' fire, because you will get burned!

Love and by: Anthony Dixon

Don't Worry
(Dedicational poem)

Baby, just sit back, relax, and don't worry;
even though, you and I both want you to
come back home in a hurry!
But, we also know that hurrying makes waste;
It makes your thoughts and visions blurry,
which leaves too much room for mistakes.
In this situation, it is best with less stress
just to be patient and wait;
While planning our brighter future,
and the steps along the way, that we will take.
Reminisce on our tender kisses,
and hugs with tight embrace.
Know I'm always your Mr.,
just as sure as you're my Mrs.
whenever you need to take your mind,
off of that place;
I'll be here,
picturing you my dear in negligee and lace;
eating chocolate candies in edible panties,
while I'm getting ready
to put a smile on your pretty face;
Romancing, and dancing
with my arms wrapped around your waist.
They say that absence makes the heart grow fonder,
and you are the one for me who fills that space!
No matter how much time, short or longer;
I believe in you with all of my Christian faith.
Just remember; no one would ever try do something,
that they knew they couldn't do;
They would only try it, if they knew they could;
and since giving up is something we shouldn't do;
It would have to be an impossible reason

why we would;
Whatever in life that we may strive for;
I believe it is always possible;
So strive baby girl, The World Is Yours!
Sweetheart you are unstoppable!

2/2/06

All About: Don't Worry

I wrote this poem when someone I knew told me that he wanted me to write a poem for his girlfriend who was going through difficult times in her life. I had told him a week before that I wrote poetry, and if he ever needed me to write something, I wouldn't charge much. Five minutes after he told me to write something for his girlfriend the thoughts began to pour like iced tea, and lemonade in the summertime! It also helped that I knew of his girlfriend, so it didn't take me that long to compose this gift. Hey, that's what friends are for! I thought about what I would tell my own lady if she was in that predicament. The same care and concern that I would show to my lady; I used in the poem to show to his girlfriend. They are both women with some things in common, so I knew that this concept would work, and work like a charm it did! He told me later that week that she received the poem, and loved it! I wasn't surprised, but I was eager to hear about her response. Women have nearly the same instincts; so by thinking and writing as if it was for my own lady, I knew that she would enjoy it.

One thing that I never had a problem with doing was putting a smile on my ladys' face! I knew it would be a breeze to put a smile on another womans' face from my expertise gained from my own relationships. That's something that I was most definitely not worrying about!

Escape

I keep trying to escape the sadness,
of this worlds' madness!
Hypocritical political views
that makes them win,
and everyone else lose!
From the few choices left,
there is little to choose;
from the outside looking in,
and on the inside feeling the blues!
Yet still - I - try to escape this sadness,
occasionally drinking away my pain
to feel happiness;
It seems sometimes it is my only solution,
in this world of pollution,
drug distribution, and execution!
So if anyone asks,
my New Years' resolution;
is to pour more drinks to the revolution!

2004

All About: Escape

I wrote this poem looking at the world through my crystal ball, as I touched on subjects that affect each and every one of us in one way or another.

I don't approve of war, drugs, and political corruption! Reality is: the sources of these problems are in way too far over my head! I mean, deeper than my pockets already are; when I'm broke, and without a penny to toss in the air to say heads or tails with! That's the system for you! Out of touch just like those millions, billions, and zillions of dollars that I've never seen, and probably never will see in my life! The only power that I have is the power invested in me, and the power of my one single vote! A vote that really wouldn't make that big of a difference anyway since no one has, or ever will win by one vote. That's impossible because those crooked politicians will be sweating so hard that they'll pay someone to fix at least one or two of the voting polls for them! Now isn't that the naked truth!

While everyone's voting, I'm going to be plotting my escape to paradise once and for all at some nude beach with my own beach house as far away from D.C. as possible! Unlike those conservatives; I don't mind showing, and telling the naked truth!

Love and by: Anthony Dixon

Faith

It allows me to be able!
It permits me to be stable!
Without haste, I wait with faith!
It makes me a believer!
With it, I grow to become an achiever!
It's what it takes to be a good listener,
a heartly giver, and a humble receiver!
It keeps me strong when the days are long,
and when the worlds ways are going wrong!
It helps me sing a grateful, faithful song,
because I am alive through God
and his faith has allowed me to continue on!

3/19/06

Feelings

Agony and pain,
torture and strain;
infamy or fame,
relevant or lame;
pathetic,- ashamed,
These are feelings that could and would,
not only ache, but break the brain;
Feelings that could draw the lines,
between sane and insane;
I try not and hope not to die in vain;
I train to maintain,
but it's not always good enough,
Life can be rough;
I can only be tough,
through hell, sleet, snow, rain,
and winds of high gusts across the plains;
The odds were against me,
and so was the grain;
but still I prevailed,
to sail again.

2004

All About: Feelings

I touched on the deep, touchy subject of feelings in this poem, because they are something that I have so many of.

Life for myself has been like a rollercoaster, and I've experienced many different feelings on my ride up, down, and all around! Everyone can relate to this subject, because we all as humans have them. Some are stronger than others, and they affect each and every person differently. Some people know how to handle them, and others let their feelings take control; which only makes them act out their feelings in an uncontrollable rage that leads them to either hurting themselves, someone else, or leaving them encaged! They later find out why the caged jail bird sings! Those that do handle their feelings, no matter the degree; don't accomplish this task easy! It can be a very frustrating process. I write to cool myself down, and to relax when my feelings are hard to deal with. Doing anything positive is the answer to solving the problems dealing with emotions, instead of just letting this rollercoaster take you for an unwanted ride.

No matter the situation; you keep it in control, and not your feelings! If you allow your feelings to control you then you will be making matters worse for yourself, and feeling worse later on when you are suffering from the consequences of your actions.

Love and by: Anthony Dixon

Fireflies

Flaming fireflies grace the sky at sight
by blinking, they give off light to the dark;
shining bright like stars in the night;
Guiding my path along with the moons' twilight;
Neon lime greens, oranges and yellows;
O' those fireflies made me
one happy and hungry fellow;
Because their colors reminded me of jello,
and whenever I was aggravated
they made me mellow;
I would just step outside for them to say hello;
and they would light up my life,
like one gigantic halo!

2004

Gods' Gift (Life)

You gave me life, even though it hasn't been easy;
It is the most precious of things!
You paved my way when I was lost,
and when I couldn't afford the cost, you paid my price;
I praise The Most High and Honorable of Kings!

My Lord up high beyond the sky,
and over the wind that blows;
Whom hears my cries, and sees my eyes
then sends his Angels down low;
To rescue me from castastrophe,
and the blasphemy of his foes!
He knows: He is the all knowing,
he is my light that always glows;
so bright that he is out of sight,
but his living waters always flow!
They seep beneath through the earth so deep,
But ye won't reap if ye doesn't sow!
I learn from your gospel;
You teach from up high, but reach me way down low;
God, thank for your gift of life,
because your love has freed my soul!

Feb. 2006

Hard Times

Laid off,
and unable to afford the costs!
Bills to pay,
and everything's on display;
but there isn't any replay on today;
So face on and move forward,
towards tomorrow;
leaving behind yesterdays' sorrow,
of having to beg and borrow;
Taking the lead,
and not having to follow;
to get through these hard times,
before they permanently scar the mind!

2004

All About: Hard Times

In this poem I expressed some of my feelings about the struggle of survival in life; dealing with the economic problems that most average, everyday people face. Layoffs, expensive cost, and bills! Believe me! They leave me no thrills!

It is indeed a struggle to manage with a regular nine to five job making minimum wage, to keep up with the expenses of day to day living. These hard times can be very rough, and if you are not prepared for them the outcome can be fatal. Preparation is key, and the earlier you start; the better off you will be! Improvise and organize a game plan to follow that will help you to know, and grow along with your account size; so you won't have to beg and borrow.

Live for today, but prepare for tomorrow; or else regret in painful hardships' sorrow!

Love and by: Anthony Dixon

Have a Heart

Have a heart!
A dollar is where it starts!
If our hearts add up to two-hundred thousand;
then we won't be thrown out into the dark;
without housing,
and no where to go and rest our soul,
because we all know that life can take its' toll;
Fore there are many people with homes,
and compared to those numbers;
the people that are homeless seems few.
But in this case, one is always too many,
because without a home what would you do?
It is tough enough alone,
and even tougher without a home!
You all have to holler if you hear me,
because I can't be reached by a house phone!
Even though the Over Flow is a shelter;
It keeps us out of the stormy weather;
when the night falls, the streets call,
and our back is against the wall;
or when there is no one else who cares
enough to be a helper!
I have a question for any misconceptions.
If you were alone, or here with us,
because you also lost your home;
Where do you think you would go,
If they closed down the overflow?
what place other than the harsh streets to roam!
How would you sleep at night
without a bed, pillow, and sheet to wrap tight?
Instead, resting your head on a park bench

without a shower, and
splashing yourself with baby powder
trying to cover up the stench!
From perspiration through your pores,
as the rain begins to pour more and more;
leaving every single inch of you drenched!
Unable to change clothes,
because your wardrobe consists of only
the clothes that you wore today and the day before;
If you ever lost anything,
or in our case lost everything;
then you can understand why!
No one is choosing to be losing;
which makes losing so sore;
So if you have a heart
a dollar is where it starts!
But if you have a lot of love to pour,
then please give more;
because we are thankful for what we've got,
So we have to stop;
the closing of the Over Flows' doors!

April 2005

Heart Thief

I didn't expect for you to stab me in my back so rapidly;
With you, I thought I had a love story,
but it turned into a tragedy!
I treated you like a queen,
and you treated me like a fiend!
You sold me a dream!
Not sharing, nor caring!
Not sparing my feelings,
but tearing my wounds,
beyond the chance of healing!
You left me not knowing when ex-loves scab
would start growing and peeling!
Though, I should have been more careful
with whom I was dealing,
because you were appealing to the eyes,
and my eyes were revealing!
You stole my love!
You should be arrested for stealing,
because not in a million years;
in all my belief...
Did I ever think I would be a victim
of a crooked heart thief!

Heart Thief Part 2

My bad nerves are the result of your bad attitude,
and bad ass curves; that made me a mental wreck
from putting up with your disrespect and harsh words
that sucked the living life out of me,
and left me for the birds;
to peck and prey on the whole day long
while you laughed, and smiled you evil devil child.
You have no compassion for your own lovers' feelings,
because you are a heart thief,
and the only thing you know about love is stealing!
You got beneath my skin and started peeling
with sins sharp end blade;
Day in and day out you rained on my parade;
then told me nothing but lies, and excuses;
Expecting me to take part in this heartless mascarade;
You wanted to hang up my death reef
you cold hearted beast!
At least now I know, so our relationship can cease
and I can once again reclaim my soul
to have true inner peace
without a seductive, destructive,
and compulsive heart thief!

7/7/05

All About: Heart Thief

I was down, out, and had the ex-girlfriend, my lady left me blues when I wrote this poem! She used, abused, and chewed me up to spit me out like bad tasting, unwanted food!

I know some of you all are like; how cruel! On the other hand; I know some of you are thinking; what a fool! To set the record straight; I feel both ways because it happened to me out of all people! I considered myself one of; if not the nicest person there could ever be, until she ruined and took advantage of me! After all the sweet conversations when I was telling her the truth about everything that I ever dreamed of, strived for, and believed; how could she do this to me?! While replying she was lying in every response, because I was one of her wants that she wanted to achieve and deceive!

To all of the sweethearts out there, if that is what you truly are: you better lock your heart up in chains and throw the key away real far! I suggest you put it in a place that is so secret that you are the only one who knows where you keep it, because a heart thief will steal it and leave it scarred!

To all of those with broken and stolen hearts, we should all just go to the police station and file a complaint on these heart thieves to make them pay, or at least replace our hearts back to the way that they were from the start! Full of love, pure, and without any marks!

Love and by: Anthony Dixon

Heartache And Pain

Uncontrollable feelings-
expressed in everyday living-
Dealing with pressure-
not wanting to settle for lesser-
I'm trying to make my situation better-
but it seems my burdens are getting heavier-
and my universal balance is getting shakier-
instead of steadier-
My patience is running out-
I'm tired of waiting and procrastinating-
I'm sick of arguing and debating-
I'm seeing not enough loving-
and too much hating-
There's not enough realness-
and too much faking-
I'm doing too much spending-
and not enough saving-
along with too much frying-
and not enough baking-
My bloodpressure's done run sky high-
from believing all of these bloodsuckers lies-
and time after time my dreams flew by-
and I could not catch one with every single try-
So bye to all of my dreams that went down the drain-
I only wish I could have you-
instead of my heartache and pain!

2004

All About: Heartache and Pain

Being that this is something that we all go through, from time to time; I decided to express my feelings in this poem describing my degree of the matter. More or less; it still is what it is! No one likes to feel it, but we all do.

Even the roughest, toughest, son of a guns that appeared to not have a heart has dealt with this issue. It could be from family, friends, your own experience, or even the loss of a loved one, or pet. I remember when I was a child and my dog past away; I was hurt tremendously! Things that we go through can affect a person dramatically. As long as humans exist there will always be heartache and pain. The facts of life are: we as people have feelings, our feelings are naturally good and bad, and life goes on. Sometimes bad feelings are brought about from the tendency for some people to cause more problems for either themselves, or for others, and in some cases both! The better that you can handle these situations; the lesser the possibilities that it will handle you on that inevitable day it comes to pay you a visit. It is up to you.

This unwanted house guest called heartache and pain can be there for only a short stay, or you can give it leeway to move in permanently; to live there for free, break you down, invade your privacy, and ruin your life until you are out of house and home!

Love and by: Anthony Dixon

Held Hostage By Society

Minimum wage has me in a cage,
and high fees won't set me free!
It is evident that I am still a slave,
and held hostage by society!
I can tell by the looks of the well paid,
and by the way they look at me;
that they can see that I am worthy of praise,
just as I see, that they are wealthy as can be!
Yet, my raise and worthy praise,
is still not raised and unreceived!
I would gladly trade places,
but he of the other race would surely not;
rather be in my position, or stand where I be;
because I have always had nothing,
and he has always had what he has got;
These are two different individuals
in two very different situations;
Ones' ancestors were conquerors with guns,
and the others' ancestors were conquered by them
to slave on plantations;
Obsessed temptations possessed
to oppress anothers' generations,
by killing, stealing, and robbing them
of a valuable education;
Creating a racist legislation,
and cracking their whips on the backs of blacks,
to speed up the building of this nation;
While mobbing and lynching in congregations,
to enforce inequal segregation;
When We the People of the United States,
for a fact, actually meant they!
That they, the whites have all rights,
to decide what everyone else should do and say!

and now four hundred years later
in an entirely different day,
they act as if nothing happened,
and everything is fine;
Hoping that we will stay;
dumb, deaf, and blind;
and ignore what went on in earlier times!
Using the excuse, I was not there!
and those actions were not mines;
Yeah, you might not have held a noose,
but those actions were surely of your kind;
The kind in which you were reproduced,
to be an heir in your family bloodline!
Your ancestors knew better,
than not to plan the outcome of their design;
by making sure when they grew old and died,
money and power would still be on their side.
They passed it down the generations,
along with slaves and plantations;
Just in case, one of theirs would cross the line,
with something like the;
Emancipation Proclamation,
that Abraham Lincoln would sign;
considering slavery a crime;
He was assassinated because he ordered,
for slavery to be eradicated and abolished completely.
Leaving the greedy,
slavemasters' of the southern states devastated!
because their schemes would be demolished!
I am thankful, but shameful,
because I am still held hostage!
Fore it has been a long time coming,
yet, there has been very slow and little progress!

Hold Me

It feels so good to hold,
and embrace another soul!
So I hope that we never break the mold
and separate; but stay together,
forever to celebrate,
because life is for us to appreciate!

5/11/05

All About: Hold Me

An ex-love inspired me to write this poem one day when I was holding her in my arms. We wrapped each other up close, taking the form of a human pretzel as I whispered gently into her ear and told her how she meant the world to me. That's when the words to this poem shortly followed. I became one with nature to express my feelings in words.

Togetherness is the cure for loneliness, and I never want to feel lonely again! I appreciated her being there, and sometimes I got overwhelmed with happiness; knowing that I was no longer alone. I tried to hold on to her forever, never wanting to let her go, because I loved and needed her so! She made me feel complete, and at the half way mark; we would always meet.

We are individually, uniquely, a couple.
Together making double the heat and intensity that generates from someone as they run, and come to hug you: for the embrace to turn into a huddled cuddle, as we both tell each other, I love you!

Love and by: Anthony Dixon

Hypnotized

I am hypnotized by your lips, eyes, hips, and thighs
By your cool whip dips and your electric slides!
You move so fluently because of your size!
You are slim like a young tree limb,
and so easy to bend over for exposure.
Your entrance is opening until closure,
as we are coming closer and closer together!
Your lower back is perfectly arched
from your posture;
I'm your bow, so behold my arrow!
Straight, long, and strong-
to keep its' composure!
Fore your path is narrow,
and I must penetrate!
Don't worry,
because I have my eye on the sparrow!
This is not a problem,
it is more like a piece of Entemanns'cake!
Because I am hypnotized,
as my arrow is lunged, taking the plunge,
centering, and entering my target bullseye!

1/21/05

All About: Hypnotized

I wrote this poem from feeling the trance of romance every time a beautiful woman is in my sight. My scope of attraction can't help, but to be locked on target! I can't help, but notice the poetry in motion of a lovely ladies' movements; swaying with the wind, teasing, and taunting my masculinity by their femininity. It's an experience that is almost haunting! To be left there in one of my memory cells; imprinted into my mind sometime long after she is gone, and out of my sight! Those memories linger throughout the night, like ghosts from a shallow grave until the morning light!

Behold the power of a woman! They are able to get my hopes up high, and keep me pushing on! They give me a reason; no matter what season, but summer is most definitely my preference. Their power and essence overwhelmingly towers over all things in the summer! Their thighs are exposed and jolting like lightning and thunder; to their own rhythm, pounding like marching band drummers! Leaving me with wide open eyes, in a daze, and hypnotized!

Love and by: Anthony Dixon

I Am

I am nothing more than I am,

Yet,- something more than grand;

I am the blueprint of civilization,

I am an African man.

March 2005

All About: I Am

I wrote this poem to signify who I am, because for some reason my name is not enough! Mistakenly, some people take me for something that I am not! They get me confused with someone else that they might have had a run into with or take me for a joke! Trying to place me in their inferior categories of what they stereotypically imagine that I should be like. That is the reason why I wrote this poem; to clear the air of the pollution of assuming, because you know what assuming does, now don't you!? It makes an as_ out of you and not me! (You have to fill your own blanks!) because I am not the one! Don't expect anything from me, but me; because I don't have to pay you any mind, or give you anything. I'm already giving enough without a choice, like taxes! Why join the army, when I am already all that I can be?! That doesn't make any sense to me! Fight for my country? I have a hard enough time staying alive and fighting unwanted battles here on the homefront. For me to come to a complete strangers defense, and work for a crooked government that doesn't care whether I live or die! They must be out their minds! I have to fight enough battles right here in my own front and back yard. This is my life and I'm the only one in charge! Not any general, captain, or sarge!

P.S. Tell Mr. No good Ole Uncle Sam that I said he better get a blood test to prove he's really my uncle, or else I'm not paying any more taxes! Ha!Ha!

Luv & by: Anthony Dixon

I Love You, but...

I love you, but...

I need a little space!

So, give me a break;

Just don't break my heart!

5/11/05

All About: I Love You, but;

I wrote this poem to free my feelings towards the situation when you are seeing someone in a relationship and they are always under you, over you, beside you, or keeping their eyes on you from a distance.

This can become a matter of pain more than pleasure very fast! There is no trust in their mind; only jealousy. That's no way to show that you love someone. I was in a relationship like that before and she was always accusing me of something that: first of all; I didn't do, because I'm not a cheater; second of all; I couldn't do, because she was always around; and last but not least; I wouldn't do, because I am a faithful man! She made every mistake in the book and expected someone to teach her the elementary fundamentals of life again! Unh, Uhh! I had to think for two people in the relationship, myself and her, and she didn't want to give me any respect, or appreciation! The sex was the only thing that kept a smile on my face, but sex isn't everything! I felt sorry and my heart went out to her at first, but then I realized that must be the game she plays to get whatever she can get from someone! She had a history of dealing with the wrong kind of men, so she didn't know what to do when the right man came her way. She tried to play it off like she knew everything, and hardly knew anything; especially when it came to love! I wish she could have just been herself. That's all I needed; without the negative attitude. Some people make simple things seem so complex for no reason. Why? Maybe only God knows.

Love and by: Anthony Dixon

I Too Had A Dream

I too had a dream like Martin Luther King,
and awakened into a nightmare of despair!
Where people are frightened and shakened,
In a world that lacks enough care!
I was founded and surrounded by poverty,
in streets that try to swallow me whole!
As negative energy and enemies follow me,
as if I hit the lottery, or hold a pot of gold!
Leaving me with no choice, but to stand bold,
so behold my voice in self defense;
When they bother me and take shots at me,
or try to clobber me to death to take my last breath,
when all I have left is my health;
Which is getting worse from the caucasions' curse,
trying to deceive us to believe that they were first;
when they were actually last, but every black childs' birth,
on this earth was told reverse in class;
When in all actuality, the only thing they were first at-

was immorality and letting a gun-blast in a niggas' ass!
So you see, I too had a dream that was shattered
by people not doing anything about the matters at hand;
Crooked politicians that were - and still are,
in the position to make a change,
when they should've, could've, and still can;--
make the right decisions, but racisms' division,
was - and is still popular by demand!
Which made matters worse to this day,
the way they still stay and stand!
God Blessed African America
with Dr. Martin Luther King;
Now We Must Keep Our Hope Alive,
and Continue to Dream!

10/26/04

All About: I Too Had A Dream

I wrote this poem plagued with the problems that exist in this modern day, so called home of the brave and land of the free; which evidently wasn't and isn't my home, land, or even meant for me!

I remember Dr. Martin Luther King for what he stood for and achieved, and it is a tragedy that our race has come to the conclusion that it has! The African on African violence must stop! I didn't state black on black, because I am not black! I am brown to be specific; and why go by a color, when you have a nationality? Nationality means people having a common origin, language, tradition, and capable of forming or actually constituting a nation state. That's what we have, so why can't we all just get along?! Some people are making it seem like Dr. Martin Luther King died in vain, but he did no such thing! There are still a lot of people who fail to realize that if Dr. King didn't stand up for our cause then; we would still be feeling the massive weight of prejudice that African people were experiencing then; right now today! A lot of the youth today have went astray down a hateful dead end road that I hope they make it back from; so that our future may have a positive outcome..

To all of the African youth; whether born in America or not, you should respect Dr. King for his struggles, visions, and dreams! He did these things for us all! Respect his purpose, cause, and effect to change the racial prejudices that he faced and fought back peacefully! The same prejudices that we would still be facing right now if he didn't act in the courageous way that he did! He was murdered for peacefully protesting against racism, so that we could go to the same schools as whites and achieve a better education.

The same schools in which; now many misled African teens organize their gangs and hang to fight in! Shooting each other in the parking lots, and spreading hatred that leads back to their own communities! The same communities that Dr. King stood up for and tried to protect from the racist harassment of segregated yesterday. Have you forgotten that was only yesterday?!
Now here you are today, going the wrong way!

You should be more than ashamed of yourselves for ignorantly covering-up his name, because if it wasn't for him; then you might not have a drop of blood in your veins! So many Africans were murdered and slain, by the hate crimes that took place in those times. Back then our people stood together as brothers and sisters when the oppressor abused and mistreated them like they were lesser! Innocently, they were only trying to make life better for themselves. Now, that life is better for us; after a long time coming, many of you are doing the opposite of what you should do and are genocidally going against the grain of our purpose.

Our purpose that many have still failed to realize!

To experience the freedom to live and be at peace in Gods' Kingdom with one another! Not the freedom to be a savage, heathen, and kill your own sisters and brothers! I pray that you will one day appreciate the breath that you are breathing! Many of our poor slaving ancestors died not knowing what it was like to be free; let alone knew what it felt like to be born free! To be able to do as they chose and very well pleased!

Then, freedom to them was only a dream or fairy tale, and slavery was a very harsh reality! A lot of brothers and sisters in prison will never know what it is like to have freedom again, because they had it and took advantage of it! How can you take advantage of something so precious? Many wonder, but it happens. It even happened to myself when I was young and naive; being a follower of negativity and not a leader of positivity in my own life; that only I was responsible for!

I was fortunate enough to get a second chance after learning a hard lesson, and turning my life around. The way it should have stayed and been in the first place. Hatred has been instilled in us from being treated with hatred, but our retaliation should not be violent or against ourselves. The times have changed and we must change with the times, or get left behind to suffer in the past!

We need to educate ourselves and each other to make a difference for change to do what is needed to make our lives, and our futures brighter and better! Our ancestors are watching spiritually, and we should not offend them any longer by hating our own! Dr. King and his righteous followers marched on Washington singing; "We shall overcome" holding hands, because our whole nationality had been, and still were being oppressed by the caucasion race. The significance of them holding hands showed the togetherness that we are in much need of today! We need to form an unbreakable bond with each other once again and stay that way! So that we may live in peace amongst each other in our own communities and raise our children right!

They may be the next presidents, congressmen and women, senates, government officials, or whatever successful kind of occupation that they choose to achieve through education, preparation, and preservation. We are in desperate need of such changes, so that a direct impact will be made in poverty stricken communities that have been neglected and overlooked by poli-crooks (political crooks) for so long! We have overcome just like Rev. Dr. Martin Luther King dreamed, but our younger generations; who haven't experienced the hatred and racism on a capital level are being steered the wrong way. Sending them backwards to live in the modern day slavery of prison and addiction, because they haven't realized that everything that glitters isn't gold! They are being misguided, but I hope they wake up and smell the dark, rich, hot chocolate and live more prosperous lives!

=

Love and by: Anthony Dixon

In This Crazy Maze

I'm tired of going through this crazy maze
of hot and hazy days!
Leading me astray down lazy ways!
Unable to make a U-turn to return
to the beginning of this stage!
I feel encaged and enraged like a slave!
Held captive by society and a prisoner of myself!
Leaving me to question my own mental health!
I soak in my tears of sorrow longing for a better tomorrow,
but it seems my soul is forever hollow;

so don't fear when you hear my voice echo in your ear,
because my soul is telling me to let go
of what I held so dear
to my heart!
It is ripping me apart from start
to finish; this pain is endless!
Hurting me on a wide scale that is tremendous!
Making my actions forever more relentless,
but I'm restraining, maintaining,
and not retaliating with vengeance!
So as a man I will take the loss,
even though it is not all my fault,
but I paid the cost one time to many!
So for now on, I'm going to keep my distance,
and show resistance to never let another woman befriend
me!

They are priceless treasures of pleasure,
but through it all they have been my worst enemy!
Causing my spirit to crawl,
and my tears to fall like Niagra!
but at the same time;
making my member rise without viagra!
They are a tender, gender of seductive backstabbers,
and behold sex is the dagger!
If I could climb a ladder
and scale way up above this hell!
I would and wouldn't even care if I fell!
Knowing it would surely put me out of my misery
of not knowing the unsolved mystery of
why true love never visited me!
They say, "love don't live hear any more,"
but I don't believe she ever did!
because I am alive at the age of twenty five,
and still without any kids!

but I don't mind!
because madam my name is not Adam!
I don't need a companion with a lack of understanding!
but if it was, I would've told Eve that I don't need a lady!
So baby, you better give me back my rib!
I only feel sorry for myself,
because a broken heart is something that is hard to help,
and it is only myself that I can forgive!
In this crazy maze!

6/11/05

Inside These Great Walls

Inside of these great walls of mines
lies infinite riches and wine.
Built by a divine spirit, his being kind;
but there lonely;
where he was the one and only.
Fore all of his modest life,
he's been looking for the right goddess to find
to make his wife.
To adorn her with diamonds,
rubies, and pearls that shined;
He squeezed ripe fruit for sweet juice,
because it pleased him fine;
Along with scuperlong grapes,
picked fresh off the vine;
These walls so great; were built by love,
and can not be destroyed by hate!
The creation of these walls of a glorious fate
were built with an in-penetrable bond,
that can not break;

Trust was my mortar!
My hands were JUST!
I built them with patience!
Not one second I rushed!
And to this day they still stand tall,
where I am protected within these great walls.

2004

All About: Inside These Great Walls

I wrote this poem to express my feelings towards loneliness, and the longing to be with a woman who adored me for being me. Not the fancy, flashy, classy, things that only dreams and fortunate realities are made of.

The pain of loneliness is almost unbearable, especially to someone such as myself; who isn't bad looking, isn't overweight, isn't ignorant, or just plain crazy; not lazy, and doesn't have any babies, or babies' mamas causing drama! These thoughts made me feel kind of insecure and looking in the mirror at myself thinking something must be terribly wrong! I wondered; are my eyes bad, and possibly deceiving me?! Is my reflection just my imagination?! Is every mirror a trick mirror, or did I just break one too many in my lifetime, cursing me times seven?!

I came to the final conclusion of, who cares! I am: who, what, and the way I am, and I don't care what anyone may think of me anymore! Besides, they aren't me! I rather be happy that I am living and able, rather than be stressing the insecurities that are depressingly making me unstable. Now I feel secure inside these great walls of mines that I have built just for those that try to get at me in the wrong way. So you can keep on knocking, but you can't come in!

Love and by: Anthony Dixon

It Isn't Over Yet

It isn't over yet,
The struggle that many tend to forget;
The lost lives, the blood, the tears,
and the sweat;
The bangs of chains, cracks of whips,
and the tightening of nooses on necks;
The violence, the silence, and disrespect;
The nation of red, white, and blue,
immorally incorrect;
Committing actions so unacceptable,
that I will never accept;
and I only get angry,
when I hear their details in depth;
but even though plenty were killed,
many still - tend to forget;
the lost lives, the blood, the tears,
and the sweat;
I can't afford to gamble,
but there's one thing I'll bet;
The struggle is long,
and it isn't over yet!

Feb. 2005

All About: It Isn't Over Yet

I was inspired to write this poem one day as I was working on a cargo ship as a longshoreman. I thought to myself how much of a blessing it is to be free and pictured what my ancestors went through to make this possible. In my mind, body, and soul they will always be remembered and never forgotten! My job composed of hoisting and rigging; sent me back in time through my mind. The braids of the wires and steel ropes resembled a noose as I watched every load of cargo carried out by the crane. I thought to myself, it isn't over yet. My imagination and fear of what if, allowed me to think of myself being on the Amistad. Dreadful thought after thought raced through my mind, as I was fifty feet down inside of the belly of this cargo ship. Thinking to myself that if this was in earlier times; my caucasion co-workers would not be working with me, but working against me. The same way their ancestors were against mines. Many of them join the bandwagon of hatred with their Anti-Christian brothers and rape, hang, and murder nearly every black woman, man, and child insight! It's not hard to tell!

I didn't have to be there, my ancestors were. For a long time war was the way of the world. I can only be a true warrior and say that it was either us or them. A warrior shows no mercy; and only honors himself! Life is about survival and people do what they feel they have to survive at their least expense. If we would have enslaved the caucasions for four-hundred years then they would be feeling the same way that we do now. We would be the majority, and they would have no choice, but to just get on with their lives.

It's just the way the table turned and they came out on top! I don't like what happened, but now and then are two different time periods. If the shoe was on the other foot what would you do? Wear it! My point made exactly! Some are fortunate and others are not, but it is not right in today for the fortunate to try to keep the unfortunate from being fortunate. I'm pretty sure they wouldn't like it if someone did it to them.

Love and by: Anthony Dixon

It's Not Hard To Say

It's not hard to say,
that I love you in every way!
It's not hard to say,
that I need you here with me to stay!
It's not hard to say;
that you make everyone of my days a brighter day,
and I'll do anything to make my dreams come true to be with you!
I'll even get down on my knees right now and pray,
and ask you to be my wife this day!
Our love is true so say I do,
so let's be on our way!

Feb. 2005

All About: It's Not Hard To Say

An ex-companion/significant other, and lady love of mine; inspired me to write this poem that I actually started singing as a song before writing it as a poem.

She filled the void in my life that I had been missing for so long. On a romantic night that her and I were together; the first two lines came to me and I started singing them. I wrote the lines down and added more to piece the song together; although I'd never ventured and explored the art of song writing. I realized it would make a great poem also, so I added it to my collection for this book. I know it is something that other lovers will easily relate to, and be inspired by in this poem of love.

Love and by: Anthony Dixon

It's Too Late Now

It's too late to turn back now!
There isn't any way,
and there is no way how!
I've made too many mistakes,
and came too many miles!
Besides the past can't be changed,
because it's done ran out of style!
I'm all grown up!
No more of being a child!
I can't change my old frowns
into new and improved smiles!
Only if I knew then,
what I do know now!
Because then it wouldn't be too late,
to prevent my mistakes,
on the long, wrong road that I went down!

5/18/05

All About: It's Too Late Now

I wrote this poem to express my feelings of making a wrong turn in life, and following that same route for so long; that when I finally realized that I had made a big mistake, it was too late to turn back and start over. I could only move forward from that point on; being very careful of my actions to prevent my situation from becoming even worse. I started down that wrong road as a child, and when I realized it; I was an adult. Too many days and years have passed, and I can't go back and relive them! The golden years are gone, and with them my first true goals that I longed to achieve. "Only if I knew then, what I know now," was a long hard lesson learned, but I still have my secondary, and third goals to accomplish. I might didn't achieve my first, but I made sure that I had back up plans!

Love and by: Anthony Dixon

Lacking Something

I have an itch, but I need a scratch;

I have a cig, but I need a match;

I have a nick, but I need a nack;

and I have a book, but I need a sack;

All these haves' but there's something I lack;

It just goes to show, that I can't have everything.

2004

All About: Lacking Something

I wrote this poem to express my feeling on the haves' and the have nots. I know how it feels to have nothing but the clothes on your back! To have one thing, but not the other; or to have alot of things and still be missing something. For instance: peanut butter without the jelly, sandwich meat without the bread, kool-aid without the sugar, and cereal without the milk! Being in a situation like this is one of those unforgettable moments that are more like a nightmare, but even worse; because it's a reality!

I have to write about this subject, because I lived to tell about it. I wasn't born rich, so I didn't have everything that I wanted and desired. I'm still not rich and the same thing goes, but if I was rich; that still wouldn't guarantee that I'd have everything that I wanted, because some things can't be bought; they must be learned, or given, because they are not material things. I appreciate what I have, and make the best out of my situation with my properties; whether material, physical, or mental, and instead of lacking something; I work on trying to have something!

Love and by: Anthony Dixon

Last Kiss

With all the valuable time invested;
you should have just let me know
that you were not interested!
That I would have respected and accepted;
but instead, you left me neglected and desperate!
Then moved on to your next
to be checked off your list!
Left me forever longing
for that one last kiss;
that I miss so much,
our lips as they touched!
In such astoundment,
causing immediate arousement!
So if dreams could come true
I would only wish,
to be with you for one last kiss!

2004

All About: Last Kiss

I wrote this poem after the break up between my double ex-girlfriend and I. It was a hard point and time in my life to get through, which I still haven't recovered from a hundred percent. I didn't know a relationship could break someone down as mines did, and I definitely didn't think that it could happen to me! I thought I was stronger than that, and believed that it wouldn't happen to someone as good hearted as myself. Good or bad karma was no help in this matter! It was just a mistake that I had made from choosing to be with the wrong kind of women. I still didn't deserve the treatment that I received, but I'm just glad the mind games that I dealt with are over with!

She was a seductive, manipulating, gold digging, want to be playa; that is a threat to the existence of mankind! She should have armed guards around her at all times to make sure that she doesn't do this to another good man! I was a victim, and I hope that this madness will come to a stop! When will women be able to realize, and appreciate a good man when he is there for them, no matter what?! Instead of realizing too late, when his heart has been shattered, and her heart is finally looking for real love that it has already had, and lost because of her cruelty. It is a crime, I say! A crime! They need the book thrown at them! This book!

Love and by: Anthony Dixon

Lord Have Mercy (Paradise In Eden)

Lord have mercy,
because the sight of you makes me thirsty,
and wanting to be quenched by your love
leaving every inch of me drenched!
One hundred percent of my brain is wondering
if you will ever pour your love
into my crying doves' trench!
So that I may be satisfied and kept alive
by your side as calm as low tide!
Fully hydrated and revived!
Feeling stronger; no longer is my mouth watering
from the thought I had pondered upon for so long
when this journey had just begun!

I'm hoping not to see a pond in the form of a mirage,
but to taste the actual grace that God
filled you to the brim with!
Low fattening like skim milk,
and smooth as silk as you sooth my lips, while I sip,
from the fountain of youth in between your hips!
There; where the proof of truth lies inside of you
about paradises' romantic rolling hills,
and clear mountain views!
Destinations beyond your imagination
that are filled with thrills and no limitations!
Entirely up to you to venture without sensor;
Where you are free, and more than welcome to enter;
The Garden of Eden from the past you are leaving
to enjoy this splendor!

2004

All About: Lord Have Mercy
(Paradise in Eden)

This poem is about my needs, wants, and desires that I feel towards beautiful, intelligent, and extravagant women; that appeal more to men than the United States Court system! I've longed for this kind of woman all my life, and I thrive on just the mere thought of them. They keep my clock ticking; they make me feel like I have something to live and love for. I don't want to leave this Earth not knowing what it feels like to indulge in the pleasures of true ecstasy and freedom of expression with some of the loveliest ladies of this planet. This is truly paradise if you can block out the violence, and ignorance that some people live for.

I imagine the Garden of Eden when I look outside

and realize this is Heaven on Earth, or at least the closest to Heaven we are going to get while we're here! So why not have a good time and let the good times roll?! Life shouldn't be dull, but full of excitement, adventure, and love!

Love and by: Anthony Dixon

Lord I Thank You

God I thank you for giving,
me the life I am living;
along with your only begotten sons'
who has risen;
up above into the heavens to be in your presence;
The Most High Almighty God in the essence,
I thank you for your blessings;
I read your word and serve as the apostles;
because I am a witness of your gospel;
You are the greatest role model,
and ultimate prime example;
You give me vision through wisdom, and your love
fills my spirit off of just a small taste or sample;
You are my light – forever bright
without the sun, moon, or candle,
and you never gave me any more
than what I could handle;
You are my Savior, The Most High Lord,
God Almighty I thank you!

Jan. 2006

Lost in the Past

A lonely soul,
lost in the past;
Speeding, trying to catch up,
hoping not to crash;
head on into the present,
before reaching the finish line of better living,
only to come in last;
Racing without pacing from the beginning,
cut out their chances of winning;
Hasting, chasing runaway dreams,
that seemed not to be moving so fast;
As they passed,
their soul followed,
thinking it was their salvation,
they forgot about planning their tomorrow;
but it was nothing, but a hungry temptation,
waiting for their soul to be cast;
So he could reveal his face,
and take off his mask;
to open his mouth that lead to a belly hollow,
where runaway dreams,
and lost destinies were swallowed!

5/8/05

Love and War

Betrayal, lies, and deceit;
tries to compromise my defeat;
The heat is immense and intense,
like hot steamy sex under the sheets;
Perspiring, tiring, and making my body weak;
to only regain strength,
enabling me to go a longer length;
after rejuvenating my love,
which power is to the tenth;
Before war comes, and tries to settle the score,
to leave the smoking, heartbroken battlefield tore;
as blood begins to pour down
into the path of wars' wrath;
creating even more devastating bloodbaths,
as love and war clashed;
Leaving remains and bashed brains stained,
on the canvas of grass blades
that were trampled by the raids;
From love and wars' deadly parade,
that left lifeless bodies laid;
Since then they were rinsed and cleansed
from the sins of those men,
whose lives were claimed and washed free of misery
by the first heavy rain that came;
to wash away the pain throughout the day,
of this site that would soon be a massive grave,
for all respects to be paid;
to these fallen masters of the art of war,
that were left in pieces; masterpieces,
To only die once, was these true warriors' thesis;
They painted pictures well,
of a yelling bloody hell;

as they fell to the ground, like a secret,
not to make a sound;
So when the painful news traveled
to their wives in town,
piercing their hearts to tear them apart;
feeling lifeless themselves,
they forcibly threw themselves down;
All know, the sighs of a widows eyes
will be filled with the tears of her cries for years;
long after losing their husband, so dear;
The fear of loneliness sets in,
like the last sun over the horizon,
because she will never see him again;
They were the closest of friends
that those women had in men;
Whose future seemed bright, but became so dim;
as they slipped into darkness's core,
to be memorialized forever in stone by love and war.

5/18/05

All About: Love and War

Love and war are two powerful forces that hate each other tremendously! Hatred is loves' enemy, and hatred loves to turn love into chaos and war. You will only see them together on the battlefield! One is fighting for righteousness, and the other is fighting for evil. This clash of warriors leaves many innocent and loving slain, and many hateful and wicked maimed! This is a fight to the death! So far, it has been never ending, and it probably will never end! Which side are you on? You can only prevail and excel by going the right way, and doing the right thing! Many have died for these causes. This war is tragic, and fierce! My respects go out to the widows and loved ones of the brave loving men and women, who died; not in vain, but to gain the respect of love from its' enemy; hatred! They knew that if respect would not be given; they would have to take it! Not knowing whether, or not if they were going to make it! Their actions were justified by a good cause, uncertain if they would fall. They would push on strong, and fight the good fight throughout the day and night; to make sure that everyone else knew that to love someone and be loved by someone is alright!

Love and by: Anthony Dixon

Love From a Distance

I love you from a distance,

because you barely notice my existence.

So every chance that I get;

I run for the opportunity

to come to your assistance.

Hoping that we will become closer,

so that this waiting period is over;

so I can love you without resistance!

5/11/05

All About: Love From A Distance

I love life, living, and everything positive; except for H.I.V. results; so beautiful women stand third on the top of my list. It isn't hard to love someone. All you have to do is be yourself and show them some love! I believe in love at first sight, because love has many different meanings. Even though I may not know a woman; I might love the way that she looks, and everything else that I see and sense about her. I love many women from a distance, but that doesn't mean that I've fallen head over heels in love for them! I just admire and feel the attraction of their beauty. It's a harmless love, unless you don't have a woman in your life!

Loneliness can lead to lust and depression in some cases of wanting without having, and wishing she was the love of your life. It has been times in my life when I've seen a lady for the first time, and was so attracted to her that I pursued this attraction even further. I wanted her to know how great of a man I was; hoping that she would become as attracted to me as I was attracted to her. I didn't want to come on to her too hard and fast, because everyone doesn't feel the same way about the same issues. I just let her know that her beauty caught my attention, as I told her about myself and inquired about her. From that conversation I get the feedback that I need to know her speed. Sometimes you and her can get up and go right out the door together, and other times you have to take it nice and slow. I had to take it nice and slow with this lady, and only could love her from a distance; waiting for every opportunity to get closer to her heart. Patience is a very valuable virtue. Especially when it pays off!

Love and by: Anthony Dixon

Love Me

Love me for who I am,
and understand that I am a man
with or without money in my hands!
Look beyond materialistic treasures
that bring various pleasure!
Then look me right in my eyes,
and tell me what weighs more
when you measure!
Materials or my life?
Fore I will never rust,
and I can always be counted on
with an undying trust!
Neither am I able to be repossessed,
and I will gain many materials
on my life long quest!
So carefully judge
when it comes to the issue of love;
and maybe you'll see
that you really should love me!

2004

All About: Love Me

Sometimes people can be so judgmental, and some people are always that way. I wrote this poem to clear the air, because how can you judge someone when you don't even know them. This happens sometimes, because the outer appearance of a person may not appeal, or be similar to anothers; which makes them judge that person to be a certain way, when they don't even know that to be a fact.

Besides, who are you to judge?! Not God!

I've been down and out, and had my ups and downs, but throughout it all, I was myself; not just a person on the streets, too lazy to get a job and support myself; nor any other names that fall under a stereotypical category. I was Anthony Dixon through it all. A human being, a person created uniquely, but share (somewhat) equal rights with all the other citizens in this country; (because we are still in need of change). On top of that I am a poet, artist, and a great basketball and soccer player. In other words, I can do some things that other people can't even do, but I'm not bragging. That is just a characteristic of myself that I practiced at and achieved. Even if you know someone, why judge them? Why not leave that up to God, because you might be the same way one day, because things do happen!
If anything, try to give them advice, help, or support.
Everyone needs it!

Love and by: Anthony Dixon

Love Must Was A Crime

I try to make things change instead of remaining the same,
because for all of my mistakes I am the one to blame!
Time after time, I was told the same lines!
Incriminated by sin!
I guess love must was a crime!
Because you took my love for granted,
and tried to chop down my rose;
when from a seed it was planted!
I was yours to hold and you took advantage
of my mind, body, and soul.
You did so much damage!
You tried to destroy me and ignore me,

when I only wanted you to explore me deeply,
adore, and amour me!
Not to annoy me, bore me, and use me for money,
thinking you were sneaky!
I tried to keep you happy,
but instead of laughing with me; you were laughing at me
when nothing was even funny!
Sadly, you took me for a joke,
and left my heart broken badly!
I should have known all the while,
and slowed down to read the warning signs!
Because I got stopped in my tracks!
Love must was a crime!

2004

All About: Love Must Was A Crime

I'm tired of falling in love when I should be standing in love, because I keep getting kicked every time I fall! As innocent as love may seem, it can have another dark, evil, guilty, and filthy side to it that portrays itself as love, but has the characteristics of lust, lies, and deceit. A side that can crush a true, pure heart that is innocent, and make it corrupt as the one that started this madness; better yet, sadness that ripped it apart. Once again, an ex was the inspiration to write this poem, even though I wish I had never endured the pain to experience such a traumatic encounter with a woman. I had a heart the size of the unknown universe that I was still exploring myself; trying to find, and get deeper into the space of love.

Give a person your heart and you are forever without it; living off of only memories, and nerves that pumped defeat through your veins. It's like being in a competition that you never signed up for, but were always up against, and challenged by the one you adored most; your significant other! Choose wisely, or live forever in agony of the tragedy that rushes rapidly to your heart and crushes it instantly!

Love and by: Anthony Dixon

Meaningless

So many things seem,-
as if they have no meaning;
Sometimes appearing so unreal,
I feel I am dreaming;
Then I find myself fiending,
for something that I had before
that I have no more;
Wishing that I had again,
so I could start brand new and begin;
to embark on a journey,
knowing how to win;
Because I've tried and failed,
but it seems meaningless to try,
and not prevail;
I just hope one day that I will set sail
with a treasured purpose
that accounts amounts,
that are far more than worthless
and my unlucky head,
turns to my lucky tail!

2004

All About: Meaningless

Understanding is something that we all have some of, and try to gain more to help us get through situations and benefit ourselves in our own lives. The understanding of some things are simple and on the contrary; others are more complex. Some things, you literally have to be a rocket scientist to figure out, when others you can ask my five year old sister and she'll tell what it's all about. The more troubling problems though, which take more thought and consideration, can cause a person to go through emotional distress from being caught between a rock and a hard place.

That's where you can find me most of the time! Trying to figure something out that seems meaningless, only to come to a conclusion, realize it's not the answer, and start over from scratch on the drawing board; to either figure it out or puzzle myself even more. I'm pretty sure that we all agree that everything has to have a meaning, other than the ones that don't care to find their own meaning and purpose in life. A reason and purpose for being. If it wasn't a reason for us being here, then why would we even exist? Some believe in luck when it comes to beating the odds of the unexplainable, but what are the reasons for those odds? Failing at trying to figure out the meaning of things in itself may seem meaningless, but without trying; what would we accomplish?

Love and by: Anthony Dixon

Memorial Day Troops Salute

Dedicated:
to all the allies, p.o.w.'s, and U.S fallen soldiers;
Who fell in the line of duty,
where no one else could have ever stood bolder;
I truly salute thee;
because: for your country,-
with honor,- you passed,
Leaving us with your memory,
that will - forever last;
Now we will honor you,
by raising flags at half mast,
because going on without you,
has been a difficult task;
So we know, we must be as strong,
and as brave, as you were in those days;
when victory was won,
and salvations' roads were paved;
In loving memory of all our American Troops;
Our heart goes out to you,
in one Great Memorial Day Salute.

2004

All About: Memorial Day Troops Salute

I wrote this poem to enter in a Memorial Day poem contest that was in a local paper in Connecticut. When I completed it, I just knew that I was going to win. I put a lot of thought and depth into this poem; which wasn't hard, because it comes naturally for me, but I was outraged when they announced the winner in a later issue. It wasn't even a poem, if you ask me. It was a prayer. Now if they said it was a prayer writing contest, then that's what I would of sent them, and mines probably would have won.

On top of that; the person who sent it in was supposedly to be serving in the armed forces in the war in Iraq, and supposedly sent the poem in to their family here in the states; who then sent it in for the contest. That's capital B.S. unless they have a time machine, because the prayer was full of old english that was used in the seventeenth and eighteenth century. So, unless they were fighting in the Civil or Revolutionary War, and had a time machine to zap themselves into the twenty-first century, then that prayer should have been disqualified. My poem on the other hand was original, authentic, best fit, and deserved to honor those who served their country proudly.

Love and by: Anthony Dixon

Missing You

I miss you,
and still reminisce on the times that I used to kiss you;
Ever since you left,
I have been having a hard time not being around you;
because when I met you,
I was so happy that I found you;
With only my love,
I wanted to drown you;
In my arms surround you,
to keep you warm and safe from harm,
so no one would hound you;
Enlighten you with charm,
I was more than proud to;
I would have loved you even more,
if only I knew how to;
because you were worth more to me,
than all the money in the world could amount to;
That is why I told you the truth,
praying that you would stay with me
so I could show you proof;
No games involved,
because most of my problems,
you were there to solve;
any disputes we had, I tried to resolve,
because you were my world that I watched revolve.

2004

All About: Missing You

My first true love on my behalf, (an ex-) provided the fuel for my fire to write this one to add to my collection. I missed her even after she left with the lame excuse that I drink too much. I never hit her, and I don't waste my breath on arguing; so what was the problem. I had a good job with benefits doing construction in the union, my own apartment, and my love was devoted to her and only her. I passed down opportunities to be with other beautiful women, for a woman who didn't know how to treat a good man.

Two years after the fact; she called me, after I had given up on love from being heart broken. She said that she missed and still loved me. The games some people play, but it's not funny if you're the one who is getting played! I caught her on her porch with another man right before we separated. We were still seeing each other briefly. She was still trying to get money, that's a gold digger for you; and I was trying to patch up the holes that she put in our relationship. I called her on my cell phone on the way around the corner from her house, and when she asked me where I was; I said, at home across town. She said, that she was doing something and that she was going to call me back shortly. We hung up and I came around the corner to see her sitting close to another man on her porch. I said hi to her, and she responded back with a guilty and caught out look on her face. I just took it in like a man, even though it hurt more than any pain that I had ever felt in my life.
I then left heartbroken, and feeling foolish myself.

I tried my best and gave my all, but to some that isn't good enough. I missed her for a long while, but regret every minute of it, because she wasn't worth it.

Love and by: Anthony Dixon

Mistake?

Sometimes I feel my life must was a mistake!
because long as I can remember
all I have made was mistakes!
Mistake after mistake!
I never got a break!
even though when I was young
I practiced to be great!
but it lead to a horrible fate!
because I made a lot of people jealous,
and they abused me hate!
Sometimes it seemed my own family
treated me like I was a mistake!
Passing me along knowing they were wrong;
making me feel like I didn't belong!
Neglecting me by not accepting me
when I was there responsibility!
Yelled at me, beat me, and tortured me with hostility!
Left me feeling like I was a mistake
that made nothing but mistakes!
Using the method of Reproducing to reap confusion!
They might as well not have giving me life
instead of making their mistake!

2004

All About: Mistakes

This poem is about how dealing with the stress that is a part of everyday life from a young age; takes a toll after a while. Especially if a childs' upbringing wasn't nurtured with love, care, and guidance; rather than just telling them to do something and expect them to do the right thing, when curiosity is a very large factor in a childs' life. Every child has dreams and goals that sometimes get short stopped by negativity around them. Whether at home, in the neighborhood, or at school; family and peer pressure plays the largest role in child development. The securities or insecurities that every child faces effects the future of that childs' outcome in life. It determines whether they will be successful or living with debts and regrets for the rest of their life.

It tells how practice can make perfect, but how outside imperfections can ruin a childs' life. Encouragement is the best thing for a child, whether they win or lose. Even if they lost; without trying how would they ever be able to win. If they are what I consider born winners, then jealousy from other peers will definitely be a problem. These chosen ones are the most vulnerable to outside forces, because so many forces are trying to cause the down fall and failure of the one's who are excelling on the top. Unconditional love is what a child needs to feel that they have a purpose in life; and also to feel like they're loved and wanted. This love assures the proper steps of guidance will be taken to help them walk up the ladder of success. If not, then they will grow old feeling like they're life is without a purpose, or that they are a lost cause, and feeling only like a mistake that their parents made.

I just hope that the generations to come aren't misled to believe the hype, because everything and everyone has a purpose. They just have to search their own souls to find it!

Mommy Always Cares, Even When I'm Not There

(Dedicational poem)

My precious son David,
My love for you is sacred;
A mothers' special gift to her son,
It is the strongest of bonds,
so strong, no one can break it,
and in between us no one can ever come;
You are one of my shining sons,
a very divine one;
Indeed one of the brightest stars,
there are;
Out of a special two,
one of them are you;
that I can see shine, no matter how far;
Just know, anytime or anywhere,
Mommy always cares;
even when I am not there!

4/8/05

Mommy Loves You (Unconditionally)

(Dedicational poem)

Happy third birthday Quintez,
and I wish you many more;
I just wish I was there to be with you,
to let my unconditional love for you pour;
Just remember, Mommy loves you,
whatever the situation may be;
Whether we are far or near from each other,
in my heart is where you will always be;
Even when we are not together,
you are always here with me;
Mommy loves you very dearly Quintez,
and wishes you a happy three;
No matter what anyone says,
you're my Quintez;
and Mommy loves you unconditionally!

Happy Birthday, Quintez! Love Mommy!

4/8/05

Monogamous

Over a hundred degrees in between us
from lust as we rushed!
To cool each other down
with ice that was crushed!
I laughed and you blushed!
You moaned as I thrust!
My love deep inside of you
protected by trust!
Just marvelous and just monogamous!
The only way this should be!
Together forever!
Preventing us from catching the virus
better known as H.I.V.!

2005

All About: Monogamous

The passion that me and my ex-lady love's shared, inspired me to write this poem. It is something special that two people who are serious about each other can practice to preserve their lives and grow old, and happily together. Romance isn't for everyone, but for those whom it may concern; monogamy strengthens the bond between two people who love each other dearly. There are alot of people in this world; along with a lot of diseases, and it isn't easy to find the person for you that will fit the script of your soul mate. Weigh out the odds, be patient, and wait to you meet the right person; or else suffer the heartache and pain that comes with jumping in and out of relationships that were going nowhere before they started. Carefully observe, because it's your life that you will preserve.

My Aching Bones

I stand with tool in hand,
all day at work until my feet hurt;
from walking back and forth-
for the source to the mold;
of great foundations in which this nation,
of the new generation will be built upon;
Children will be educated,
in buildings – I helped to be created;
Some of the stepping stones,
that they walk up on,
will be from the hard work,
of my aching bones!

2004

All About: My Aching Bones

My pride in doing construction inspired me to write this poem. Construction is very creative, and it amazes me. To start from the foundation; seeing nothing but the space around it, and then a year, or years later there's a large school or building that will be occupied by people; where there was old houses, trees, and uncut grass there before. I loved being a part of that experience. It made me feel good inside, and it also paid very well. I think about my hard work paying off and my aching bones from my hard work, helping to build a school that children who haven't even been conceived yet will attend in the future. We as a people should be more constructive and creative to allow that great feeling inside to come into our hearts and souls. I think about how the Egyptians built the pyramids thousands of years ago, and it is still a mystery to modern day scientists of how they were built. I am proud of my achievements, especially when I enjoy myself while I achieve them. Now I guess that I'll go and soak my aching bones in the bathtub and get a back rub; peace!

Love and by: Anthony Dixon

My Heavenly Love (God Sent)
(Dedicated to Natasha)

My love sent from heaven above;
Hold me tight throughout the night;
Shower me with kisses and hugs.
I promise to keep you out of harms sight;
Help me make the right decisions with precision,
and guide me through this not so easy way of living
with the love you are giving;
You are worthy, you deserve me,
preserve me until the sun has risen,
and I am out of the dark;
Stay with me in ecstacy, my dreams, and visions
and care for my wounded heart;
I love you my love,
I want you to know that I always will;
Until the end of time is mines,
when your love I can no longer feel;
Allow me to lay in your bosom,
and rest the night away;
My sweet love sent from heaven above,
from you I will never stray.

10/2/05

Anthony Dixon

Naptime

It's naptime, but a place and time to take one
is so hard to find;
Ever since I've fell into this trap,
I can't remember the last time I've taken a nap;
so that my peace of mind may still be intact!
It's snack time, but I don't have a dime,
and no food on which to snack;
The pains in my stomach,
are joined with the pains in my back;
Along with the pains in my chest,
from the rest that I lack;
It's fact time,
because so many lies are told, that no stories exact;
and I am put on hold,
when there should be no holding back!
Then I'm being giving the dumbfound runaround town,-
finding myself at,-
the same place that I started from scratch,
Now I'm tired and I just wish that I could take a nap,
so I find myself trying to recline and lean back;
and rock away into a dream in the mid-part of day,
on a bench or on a bus, no matter where I'm at;
nodding off, body weak from getting the kind of sleep,
they named after a cat;
Sometimes my eyes are so tired,
I wish I was blind as a bat;
at least then, I wouldn't have to open my eyes,
so I could get peace of mind and take a long nap.

2/18/04

All About: Naptime

I wrote this poem while dealing with the pressure and stress that came along with being homeless, and feeling like I was without anyone who really cared around. It definitely took a painful and agonizing toll on my mind, body, and soul from not getting the proper amount of sleep. I wrote most of this book while I was homeless, and typed it up where ever I could. From the lack of rest; I would find myself waking up after dosing off briefly at a computer. How can you do anything without the proper amount of sleep, transportation, and positive support? How long can a persons' clock keep ticking after taking such of a licking? Only the strong survive, but this is a weakening dilemma. I didn't like to take naps when I was younger, but I could really go for one right now! Strange how you don't know what you have until it's gone!

Love and by: Anthony Dixon

Never to Return

Exiled,
thrown out projectile,
treated like a stepchild;
Lucifer cast out of heaven,
down to earth as a reptile;
Never to return,
forever to burn and learn,
an infinite lesson from a judgment,
that will never be overturned;
Banished, vanished, and hexed with a curse;
and hardly a soul is even concerned;

Meanwhile in St. Elsewhere,
kidnapped orphans are starving from
the malnutrition of real love;
from being caught and brought into traps
where they're forced to perform obsene sexual acts,
by pimps that substitute real love to prostitutes
until there is no coming back;
Disappearing without leaving a trace,
other than the memories of their angelic face;
the purity of their smile and grace will never return
to this time and place,
in the same form or shape;
leaving them in the state of not wanting to awake!

Never to return;
to this paradise lost,
and paying of an expensive cost;
My soul is tossed and turned;
When I suffer a loss my eyes are water glossed,
because for what I had, I still yearn;
I'll miss your kiss and holding hands;
I just wish that we didn't have to return back to sand;
Yet, I still stand firm to spend my term
here on land as a man;
Until the day that I fade away,
and these words I can no longer say…
Bye, big, beautiful world!
I am gone! Never to return!

4/21/05

Pain

In order for me to gain,
I had to endure pain;
In every shape, form, and fashion,
shamed, and blamed,
stoned, beaten, and caned;
yet, still I remained sane;
I maintained through the storms rain,
pounding on my brain;
and after work - my body hurt,
from pulling heavy chains;
I tried to fight this arthritis,
along with headaches migraine;
but in order for me to gain,
I had to endure pain.

2004

All About: Pain

This is a subject that we all can relate to, but none of us like! It is a feeling that we have all experienced in some way or another. There are many different ways to feel pain, but there is only one form of pain that men and women in particular, don't mind. That is the pleasure and pain of eroticism, but I am not referring to that type of pain in this poem. I'm referring to the pain of struggling to survive and succeeding in life. The stomach pains you get from being hungry without money for food; the body aches and pains that you feel after a long, hard days work; the pains that you feel when you lose a loved one to violence or natural causes; the mental, emotional, or physical pain that you feel from being abused; whether verbally or physically, the pain of heartbreak, and the memories of pain that still linger long after you have overcame the pain. The memory of the pain as you cried in the rain with no where to go and everyone to blame! I'm talking about the pain that you had to go through that makes you the person that you are today. The external characteristics and traits that shaped and molded you into the strong, or weak individual that you are today.

There are both good and bad pains. The good pains you have to go through to achieve your dreams, and the bad pains you have to try to avoid; because they will stop you from believing and achieving anything! Joy and pain are parts of life, but don't let your pain stop you from being happy, because life is the greatest blessing of all!

Love and by: Anthony Dixon

Passion

Imagine passion bursting into untamed flames,
and thirsting for oxygen, to trigger bigger explosions!
Before release feel the heat increase;
good grief, what a relief!
At last, true inner peace!
You're Heaven in my eyes!
The creation of a great manifestation,
and pleasant are your thighs!
I've long been waiting to reach my boiling point
of 212 degrees fahrenheit, and holding steady;
your oven is ready; my load is heavy,
and I already feel the thrill within my joints!
As it spills to fill your mold that will hold,
and yield our seed; Birthing a new generation!
The big bang theory rein-acted with fire and fury;

plus lust creating star dust;
This is more than just a demonstration!
This is creation of a revolution advancing;
leaving young stars dancing
to the rhythm of the solar system!
While giving them wisdom!
I can see through to their vision!
Hot like passion from the sun as it comes to be risen!

1/20/05

All About: Passion

The passion that I have for life, love, and romance carried the pen; as I jotted down the words to this poem. I connected the thoughts of passion and creation together showing the beauty of life, and the universe. It is a poem to mentally vision as the words unfold in your mind. It reminds me of the first time: when the heavens and the earth was created. I also connected the relativity of the creation of life to the creation of the universe and its' process of evolution.

Passion is a very deep and intense feeling brought about by a strong attraction and desire. This is the way that I feel about life. I love to live it and desire to live it happily. The world is my girl! We've got a love jones going on!

Love and by: Anthony Dixon

Perfection

Perfection is my reflection, no exception;
just acception of lifes' blessings, from conception,
through life, to death, and the resurrection;
by the manifesting of my energy through divinity,
spirit free, Allowing me to be,
anywhere in the world that I want to be;
Free to travel the seas to see all my eyes can see;
while riding on the waves, sailing through the days,
capturing everything within in a gaze,
of glory in a blaze;
Being touched by the suns' rays,
warming my system, clearing my vision,
sharpening my intuition and enlightening my wisdom;
while reflecting my prism of ones' self,
bettering my health, prospering my wealth;
and leaving my reflection, flawless perfection.

2004

All About: Perfection

A lot of people say that no one is perfect except for God. Some people make being perfect seem like such of a big deal; when others just strive for perfection for self benefit, to be better than their competition, or to just live healthy lives. Nothing is wrong with that, but those that practice to make perfect still get criticized. Critics whisper, " look at them, they try to be so perfect," or "they think that they are all that!" My opinion is, maybe they are. I don't feel that God created me with any flaws, or imperfections. If he is perfect; then so am I! He created me! Even if I am just an image of him; then I am in his perfect image. I don't believe the hype of what I am told or read. I have my own mind, so I do my own thinking. It sounds reasonable to me.

I'm comfortable with my opinion, and comfort is something that I love to experience. So tell those player haters that if they don't think they are perfect then fine, because they are only criticizing themselves and trying to block out their own human insecurities that aren't allowing them to see themselves through Gods' eyes to reveal that they are actually his children and created in the images of Gods and Goddesses. They should stop hiding behind a mask, and show the beautiful beings that lie inside of each and every unique individual.

Love and by: Anthony Dixon

Personal Problem

You say that you need this, and that you need that!
Sounds to me like you have a personal problem!
Telling me that you don't need another father,
but at the same time telling me your needs!
I don't know why I even bothered!
Maybe because I cared;
I gave you what I could spare!
But only if I knew that when I needed you the most
you wouldn't be there!
You cheated on me and to me you lied,
but it took a long time for me to finally realize!
I tried to let some things slide!
Not to say anything and swallow my pride,
but instead of keeping silent
I should have opened my mouth wide!
Because I know now that you didn't care
about how I felt inside!

I should have known all along
that I should have just left you alone
for you to deal with your own-
personal problems!

2004

All About: Personal Problem

One thing about an ex; they have a way to leave an unforgettable impression in the mind of the person they were with! I would never tell someone something if I knew it wasn't for their own benefit. I wouldn't want anyone to do that to me, so why do it to someone else?

Everytime that I showed care and concern regarding their decision making, they told me that they don't need another father. Who does, when you already have one? No one can take a fathers' place! I was just telling her good advice from experience. I didn't know something so valuable could be so offensive, but I realized in the long run that I was the one who was really being offended. I should have become as defensive as they were; putting up their defensive block to ignore everything that I said; stopping the ticking of the clock in our relationship. Time ran out, and I lost by a landslide; that includes everything, and almost my mind!

I should have known better than to try to be with someone who had nothing to offer me, but headaches. It wasn't like that at first, but as soon as they started dishing them out; I should have dished them out of my life for good! I should have at least stopped trying to deal with them on a serious level. They had too many issues, and I had enough problems of my own; but we could have worked them out together if they were for real about being together. I felt sympathy for them sitting on their pity pot, and reached out to them with loving arms. They then embraced me with the merciless grip of a python! My valuable advice to you is: Stay away from suffocating relations, unless you are going to squeeze them the same way; or else become an almost breathless, lifeless, victim of the circumstance of bad romance!

Love and by: Anthony Dixon

Possible Through You

I know anything is possible through you;
My Most High King that annoints Angels to sing;
I praise you,
and pray to know you like the Apostles knew you;
With very strong belief in your amazing grace,
I know that I can overcome any obstacles through you,
because when I look at my mirror image;
I get a vision and almost perfect picture of your face;
I savor the taste of the heavenly blessings
that my Savior gives me as I learn my lifes' lessons
destined for what you have in store for me,
and that's so much more;
because through you, all things are possible!

3-18-06

Rain Dancing for Dark Clouds: Tears from Heaven (Part 2)

Dark clouds, roaring loud, and rolling black and proud!
Holding rain that's about to start pouring
to cool and calm down the rowdy crowd!
Once the bottom of a cloud falls out of the sky
from this heavenly waterspout;
it washes away heartaches tears
in the eyes of those who cry,
and fills summers full of cheer
when it cures the driest droughts!
It wets and gets peoples' attention instantly upon release
of natures' prevention mechanism
that cools down the earth;
which is hells' holding cell,
and douses out the fire of the beast!
From the core it burns like the rising sun in the east,
but the rain on the devils' parade causes its' negativity to cease;
opening a floodgate of peace!
When the rain stops, I'm going to do a rain dance
to make the bottom of another dark cloud drop!
So people will go back into their houses
reducing the sound of gunshots within our inner city blocks!

6/29/05

Reflections

The very first time that I gazed into your eyes
I saw the sun, and only when you would come
it would rise!
As you broke through the clouds of my dark gray skies,
your shine cleared my mind and made me wise!
You greeted me with peace as well as pride;
expressing the most beautiful smile, impossible to hide!
It was peaceful as a walk along the vast countryside,
or standing barefooted on a jet black, sandy beach;
while watching the oncoming waves of mornings' tide!
You cast reflections of perfection seen far and wide,
across the calm ocean waters where seagulls glide!
You are my light and also my guide,
taking me along on a romantic ride
to a place where weds are locked and knots are tied,
and aisles are walked with a graceful stride!
So walk with me hand in hand and side by side!
We can live happily ever after as husband and bride!

December. 1998

All About: Reflections

I wrote this poem when I was eighteen years old and serving time in jail. I was attracted to a female correctional officer there; that I lusted for from my lonely world inside of a jail cell. I was serving a year for possession of cocaine with the intent to sell. A mistake that I made; that totally changed my life around. I corrected myself from being inside of those walls with nothing but time to think about my past mistakes. It was a tough way to learn a lesson, but it worked. That's all that counts to me now. I'm just glad that my time is over with of doing ignorant things without thinking about the consequences that lie ahead.

The lady C.O. that inspired me to write this poem was a beautiful, older lady in her mid-thirties, with a body of a goddess. She wore contacts in her eyes, and when she did her shift checks of the cells; she would come and look in the cell through a hole cut out of a thick sheet of plastic that was eye level, and I would be right there to look into her beautiful, brown eyes. They looked like they were on fire and full of love; love that I felt I needed so badly. I wrote the poem and gave it to her, and she came back later to compliment me and gave me an orange. I cherished that orange for days before I even ate it! I just looked at it and admired it while I thought of her for almost a week, until I decided to eat it.

I waited until my cell mate went to sleep late one night, because I didn't want him to jeopardize her job by running his mouth, because he sure wasn't getting any! He thought he was a big willy, drug selling, tough guy, but he wasn't that bright at all. It figures! I had to help him do some math problems to some drug equations that called for units of measurement to be converted into a different unit of measurement for the answer to be figured out. I was so tired of hearing him say the wrong answers! He really thought he was a bully or something though, but he didn't know I could fight, plus I knew a little bit of street martial arts that I learned from a friend who was advanced. (Someone killed him because he was so much of a threat when it came to fighting, God bless his soul). My cellmate had a heart condition on top of a nasty attitude, so I refrained myself from getting into a physical confrontation with him.

I wasn't trying to be in jail any longer than I was going to be already; for reacting in violence towards an adult who acted like a child and didn't know his basic math skills. It wasn't worth it, and he wasn't either. I peeled the orange, and as I ate it; I took out each seed. It was a very sweet, but seedy orange; and when I finished I counted each seed. There was exactly eighteen seeds, which was surprisingly alot of seeds to me, and also mysterious, because my age was exactly eighteen. I felt it was meant to be, and I guess somewhat of a message from God. To that special lady out there, somewhere; Thanks for the orange and the valuable lesson within it. You will always be remembered.

Love and by: Anthony Dixon

Regrets (Only If I Knew)

After many days of wandering astray,
remembering childhood years,
that I would often play;
Hearing it all, having nothing to say,
praying that everything will be o.k.;
My grandmother always said,
a hard head made a soft behind;
Only if I knew, that I would find that out in due time;
She also said, " You made your bed, so sleep in it",
only if I knew, the mess I would get myself into,
that I would be so deep in it;
When there was a bad storm, she used to say,
be quiet and let the Lord do his work;
only if I knew the more that I stayed quiet,
the more the pain that I felt inside was going to hurt;

Now I realize that I should've done,
more than listen to every word she said,
like thinking about and heeding those words instead;
because those words of wisdom that I did not heed,
lead me to times in my life that were full of dread;
But if I could do it all over again, there's one thing I'll bet;
I'd do whatever it takes, to live without these regrets.

2004

All About: Regrets

Every one makes mistakes that they regret either right afterwards, or later on in their lives. The worst thing about a mistake is once it's made you can't go back and change the past. It has already happened, and there's nothing you can do except for learn from it, or burn from it. My family; particularly my grandmother used to tell me about things and situations that I didn't think concerned me, or I thought that they couldn't and wouldn't happen to me. I was young, energetic, and thought that I was in complete control of my life and headed up the ladder of success. I didn't realize then how hard it was to be an adult, and take care of the responsibilities that came along with being one. I was so anxious to grow up so that I wouldn't have to follow the strict rules that my family governed me by. Peer pressure and the yearning to spread my wings to be free propelled me to rebel against my grandmothers rules, and every other guardian in my life.

When it finally came time that I was old enough to leave from under the wings of my family; I wasn't ready to leave. I didn't know what to do, or where to go. By then I had realized that my curiosity; which lead me to explore the streets, also lead me to see that nothing was out there! Nothing but the roads that lead to different places that had nothing good to offer me, but the same things that my family did; and that's rules, regulations, and the consequences of those rules if I didn't follow them! I went on going about the wrong way growing up, because I didn't prepare myself for that vital point and time in my life. I was too caught up in having fun and doing things that I didn't have any business doing. Leaving me to only regret those mistakes later on in my life.

To all of the younger readers: Don't rush to get old, because death is the next stage after old age! Cherish every moment and day of your youth and carefully plan for the day that you will have to take care of yourself. Preparation is key and leads to longevity, and prosperity.

Love and by: Anthony Dixon

Sacrificial Love

I sacrificed my love,
and it was crucified on the cross besides Jesus!
Either we seize the opportunity,
or the opportunity will seize us!
The world is full of cities under siege,
controlled by government officials of high prestige
that are ruled by greed!
People are talking about Holy Wars,
but when it comes to God;
how many really do believe?
When most try to lie and deceive,
and stop others from reaching their goals to achieve;

God gave his one and only son for me;
when Jesus sacrificed his life on calvary
so that I wouldn't have to pay an eternal price;
That is the Most Highs' might at the highest of heights
that nothing can rise above,
because the Father and Son cared for me
with a special, sacrificial love!

March 2006

Shattered Dreams

I sit here still like a winters' chill
without the wind to even accompany me!
Some people often glance my way
as if there was really something to see!
When I look at them, I see nothing but passers by!
Only there for a second,
then gone in the blink of an eye!
The ones that succeeded and weren't defeated
giving life one heck of a try!
I remember doing the same
striving for fortune and fame,
but the cost of my loss was more than I gained!
I was the best at what I did as a kid,
but life was more than a test of skills in a game!
Strange how it happens to the best of us!
The ones most qualified denied,
and the prizes are given to the rest of us!
Even though,
I'll never stop thinking of playing on the team!
Fore my thoughts are caught in the regrets,
and the nets of shattered dreams!

March 2005

Simple

It is as simple as 1,2,3 for you to be with me!
All you have to do is love,
care, and share responsibility!
Cherish, dedicate, celebrate, and appreciate;
life and love which is so great!
It isn't hard, because all you have to do is try!
It is just as simple as the blink of an eye!
There is nothing complex about being your best,
and from being so, you will pass every test!
With honor, respect, and also integrity;
and gain so much with such simplicity!

2004

All About: Simple

Sometimes people have a tendency to make things that are easy seem so complex. For what reason? I don't know, but I am full of ideas. Maybe things that come with ease are not enough of a challenge for these people. I learned my lesson the hard way from doing things the hard way, just to prove to myself and others that I could do it. That way of thinking eventually caught up to me. Now my body feels like I've been run down by an army tank from putting myself through unnecessary tests of strength and agility. Since then, I've been looking for the easy way out of doing everything. I'm only twenty four years of age and my mind and body feels ancient! I guess that's what I get for trying to grow up so fast, before my time. I was inspired to write this poem by the same beautiful woman, whom I fell in love with, but she said that she didn't want anything, but a regular friendship. As simple as it may sound, it was hard for me to understand why she was making things so complex for me. I was willing to walk the face of the Earth for this woman, and all I received from her was rejection. How could I possibly just want a friendship with a woman that I was so attracted to, and always thought about.

She inspired me to write some of my greatest love poems that I gave to her; along with my heart. I gave her this poem to make it plain and simple how easy it was to be with a gentleman like myself, but all she could say was, she's not interested. You've got to be kidding me! I guess I belong in the book, the hopeless romantic; which I am going to write in the future. I fit the script for that star roll by far.

So look forward to the book, The Man of Your Dreams Was A Hopeless Romantic Because No Woman Ever Believed In Him; in the future, to get the details of how an intelligent, strong, talented, and hansom young man; the perfect dream guy; could not find the perfect dream girl to love, and make his life complete; which tormented and tore his life apart.

Love and by: Anthony Dixon

So Long

So long, you're gone, and I won't cry!
To all of my many years
that have already went by!
I can only pray for another day,
so another ray of sun may pierce my eye!
Giving me the strength to go the length
that is so long; I must be strong!
Through joy, pain, sleet, rain;
with pride, and without shame!
To change, and never stay the same!
On my journey through life that I hope is long!

2004

Soul Mate

All my life I waited and wondered where you are!
Just in case you were in a place
where the distance was very far!
I apologize,
but I can not hesitate or wait for you any longer,
because my feelings for you can not grow any stronger!
They are weakening by the emptiness that I feel inside!
From the lack of your presence I have swallowed my pride!
I once wished upon a star for your love,
but it was never answered!
Now without you, I am dying slowly as if I had cancer!
So I can only pray to the good Lord up above,
because repeatedly I look out windows
and open doors to see if you're there!

Only to welcome in silent winds and cold air!
I no longer care! Why should I?
When you are never there!
You were the crown jewel of a king in my dreams!
A queen too good to be true it seems!
So I must move on to face the early dawn in the morning!
Once again, I am without you friend!
I've long been ran out of patience, and the precious time
that I have wasted has left me disgraced!
If true love was a promise; then she was two faced,
and showed me nothing but hatred!
A black widow in disguise that spun deception in a matrix!
Injecting her venom until I could taste it!

I admit that I was sprung
by the words that came off the tip of her tongue!
I believed she was sweet, but my perception was tainted!
Which were all in her plans to get more acquainted!
Just as sure as I was lured into her web of ebony legs
that drove me to the edge; that was as sharp as the pain
from her fangs inside of my flesh deeply wedged!
Now my head hangs in sorrow
fore I know I will not live to see tomorrow!
I just hope that I have not mislead anyone to follow
me to this bloodsucking death that left me hollow!
I now know why she wears on her back
the once mysterious symbol of an hour glass,
because once bitten your heart slows its' rhythm,
and that hour will be your last!
Life was my most prized possession,
yet death was her obsession!
Killing my feelings by using her attraction as the weapon!

2002

Spoken Portrait of a Queen

She is my everything!
The birds that sing, the bees that sting,
the breeze over the seas, and through the trees;
so my bended knee is given to thee,
fore she is free, and independently saying to me;
I am Queen!
Feel my power as I make your cream of the crop
rise to the top unable to stop flowing, growing,
and seed sowing while she's reaping the seasons harvest
every single second and minute of the hour!
Visualize yourself in between my cultivated thighs!
Then feast your eyes on I, and become mesmerized
by my detailed features!
Her body language is speaking to me, and saying
that if I am not familiar then she will be my teacher!
Come and tease her,
then please her body as soft as fur!
Be a gentleman, stroke her kitten and hear her purr!
The Royal Spread in between her legs
could make a poor man beg, and a rich man poor
for coming back to many times for more,
or an insane man use his head!
This is why she is my everything!
My Spoken Portrait of a Queen!

2/7/05

All About: Spoken Portrait of a Queen

An ex- lady love and every other beautiful lady that I have ever encountered inspired me to write this poem. I just had to capture their essences in one of my greatest talents of writing. The beauty and power of a woman is extraordinary. Women are like magnets, and men are like metal objects when they pass by; drawn in and attracted. My woman means everything to me, and without women this would be a gruesome world. I don't even want to picture the thought of it! My spoken portrait of a queen describes in perfect detail how beautiful and powerful she is. Open your mind and vision the essence and presence of these goddesses of love. You can't miss or resist this opportunity to be with them in unity.

Love and by: Anthony Dixon

Springtime

Spring makes me want to sing
as I hear the sounds of wedding bells ring
while watching the birds, bees, and butterflies cling
to the flowers, and honeysuckles to drink
the sweet nectars of life;
to then buzz and flutter by
graciously like a bedtime lullaby
and rocking in the wind,
Oh, how I love when spring begins,
because once again the weather is warm,
and turning me on with Aprils' showers,
Mays' flowers, and Junes' thunderstorms;
People are vacating for Spring Break vacations,
and leaving empty college dorms!

Leading to wild beach parties
where guys and girls are being naughty
from drinking Tequila and Barcardi Limon!
Dancing in the sand, looking for a fan in the crowd
to grab their hand to tell them to come on,
and be their new Springtime fling!

5/15/05

Stranger In My Eyes

You're just a stranger in my eyes;
I keep telling myself time after time,
but your face seeming so familiar,
and your movements so peculiar,
as if you were mines!
Maybe in a past life;
Presently leaving me wondering
if you will be my future wife?
Even though, I unpleasantly doubt the possibility
for that to ever be,
because I always find myself weighing out the odds
for one more fish in the sea!
When there are so very many, and so little time;
I keep hoping to find the right catch
to make a perfect match that's one of a kind!
So many to choose from, but I know for me
there is only one!
One stranger that will become a friend,
then companion, and eventually my lover in the end;
by letting her love pour in!
So until the day that I gain my prize
they will all merely remain just strangers in my eyes.

2/7/05

Stupidity

Truthfully there is no excuse for stupidity,
when ignorance is the cause of it all;
and the reason why people fall!
They fail to tell the time,
when the end is near, and the world is full of fear!
Chaos, dictators are living above the law,
which is the cause of every flaw;
because when they are supposed to correct they neglect,
only caring about their checks!
Then are the first ones crying,
when people start dying,
because sniper's on their steps!
Red Alert! Intense humidity! Society is hurt!
It's already hard as hell without a job,
and seems even harder to find work!
But that's no excuse for this stupidity;
so when it backfires in the faces,
of these backstabbing liars and people in high places;
Who's going to tighten the loose screws,
when they fire, the last standing handyman with the pliers?
Who knows? He might just quit;
after the government tries to take away,
or make him pay, for his own health benefits!

2004

All About: Stupidity

I wrote this poem to speak out about the social and every other kind of injustice that crooked politicians put a cover up on, and try to give the people a reasonable excuse. Then the excuse does not make any sense, sounds totally stupid, and is obvious that it's the wrong thing to do. This poem talks about how greed is causing people to neglect their responsibilities and do other than what they supposed to do in office and the hard working, tax paying people end up paying for their mistakes. It is not fair, not right, and not the smart thing to do, but they continue to do it anyway. After a while of ripping off the innocent, needy people of their district; their scams usually backfire right in their faces after the F.B.I. gets enough evidence to make sure that they will be doing the jail house rock for a good while.

It never happens though because they always get off the hook from doing big time, because of who they know and who they pay. That's the way the crooked system works! It's funny though, how these officials act like they're so concerned about the people and their communities; to only get caught mishandling and stealing money from the same people who voted for them. It's a crying and dying shame! I'm glad that I don't need their help, because I know I wouldn't get it anyway. They are too high up on the scale for my life to be affected by them positively, unless they were actually doing what they were supposed to do in their office position. Make a positive change for us all!

Love and by: Anthony Dixon

Summer Breeze

Summer breeze, where did you go?
Because I miss your touch instead of snow;
I remember I wished that you didn't leave.
The day that you left anyway,
and took the leaves that were on the trees;
You left them bare without a care,
then came cold air instead of fair!
Your touch is rare; one of four,
so when you left, I desperately begged for more!
The next time you come knocking
I'll hurriedly open the door
to feel the warm summer breeze that you have in store;
Fore you are the reason that I wait three seasons!
You never fail;
your greetings are always pleasing;
So until the next time that we'll be meeting;
I'll be looking to the trees,
for you to return my warm summer breeze!

2004

Sunrise

As I awaken;
born to a new day,
I thank you Lord for this blessing,
fore you have made me a way!
You've guided me through the darkness
in the midst of the night;
to surprise me with your sunrise,
as you showed me the light!

Feb.2005

Sunset

This is a day that I will never forget;
The first time that I looked into your eyes,
and watched the sunset;
We kissed in unison with the sun and horizon,
and created our own flames
as our temperatures started rising;
Natures' way to demonstrate,
A perfect double date;
You and I,
with the sun and the moon as his mate;
So as he ended the day and started to fade,
We laid, covered in the warmth of dusks' shade;
Then made passionate love,
to the oceans' serenade;
With waves encoring at high tides' stage.

2004

Tears From Heaven

Tears from heaven;
rain, fall from the sky;
Better to fall from a cloud,
than fall from my eye;
Rain, fall down and cool off the tempers in town;
before these hot, over crowded blocks,
are alarmed by the sounds,
of gunshots leaving flocks of people stampeding;
Breathing hard and scared,
not knowing if they are scarred or bleeding;
from shock, not really knowing what happened,
because all of a sudden,
someone thugging started clapping;
Which left only a few options for a person to do,
in this situation, it is so sad but true;
To either duck or run before a bullet hits you;
Along with, praying and hoping,
to make it out of this predicament;
Lord, I just want you to know,
that I'm so, so sick of it;
So tears from heaven, send your blessing,
and please get rid of it;
Before once again, the ignorance begins;
Leaving the permanent impression of the demented,
imprinted in the minds of the innocent;
Where the two questions lie;
Why? and who did it?
Maybe one reason,
but no excuse to grab your gun and shoot;
is that we're in the hottest season of summer,
when the heat waves are blazing,
sending anger raging,

and leaving attitudes rude with hunger;
Causing the crime rate,
to steadily rise with the temperature;
Contagiously spreading to brothers and sisters,
an undaground fever;
So tears from heaven pour on the poor,
so their tempers won't soar and lead to an uproar;
Whether bully or wimp, whore or pimp;
you are not exempt, no matter if you are rich or poor;
because when it's hot outside;
The lions and lionesses of the African pride;
in baggy jeans and tight dresses,
might be preying on your hide;
By any means to survive, I am staying alive;
Without the need of any jive turkeys
that eventually get slain for Thanksgiving dinner;
Fore I am a winner and more than worthy,
and only thankful to God for lifes' blessing,
and also his loving that is as sweet as Hersheys' Kisses,
as the remnant reminiscence of myself
doing the dishes, came back into existence
of taking the time to see the cleanliness of my mind
in the reflection of my face on my plate before I ate
Gods' grace and good food that I had to taste
without haste I wait, and thank Great God Almighty;
fore he is the one who chose to create,
and not forsake me;
As he rains down his tears from heaven,
that he sends as a blessing
to prevent subsequent violent afflicting pain,
by washing all of that ignorance down the drain.

12/22/04

All About: Tears From Heaven

I wrote this poem expressing my feelings towards the African on African violence that is taking so many young and old lives across the world. It is a shame that we are taking our anger and pain out on each other, when it was started and afflicted by another race. Not that we should take it out on them either, because it is a new time and day; and we have already overcame the mainstream prejudices that plagued our race for so long.

I lost my first oldest cousin to black on black violence and I know I would have preferred it to rain from a cloud to prevent him from being outside that night, instead of me having to cry from his death. I wished those Tears From Heaven would have rained instead of me enduring the pain of his life being slain. It isn't hard to tell, or for me to understand what is going on. It is premeditated homicidal genocide. Reverse psychology working on the minds of the slaves' free ancestors to do the white mans' will, without them even having to be directly involved. They just sit back and turn on the news and laugh as we are killing each other off. They have divided and conquered the nation of African people, and until we all realize this and put a stop to it; they will continue to win this race war that they started a long time ago that is still taking place behind societies' closed curtain. Come together and unite! To stand up for what is right! It is the only way that we will be able to positively impact our own lives and communities.

Love and by: Anthony Dixon

Temptation

You simply tempt me,
to pour my heart out to you generously;
My love is a flowing waterfall connected to your sea;
It will never go empty;
My loves' current is hatreds' deterrent;
Creating a mistic mist,
connecting to your firmament;
Your eyes can't resist this captivation of bliss,
and if your thoughts are pure;
then you will not miss the kiss
of Heaven passing down a blessing
in each and every direction;
Handed out by Gods' Angels
at the cross roads' intersection;
I often vision of this re-creation of creation,
and know it is true love,
and far beyond your imagination;
It is heaven sent from up above;
outweighing the strongest temptations.

March 2005

All About: Temptation

Another ex-lady love was my inspiration to write this poem. The strong feelings that I had for her made me feel so many different ways that sometimes I didn't even know exactly which feeling, or emotion it was that I was expressing. I usually say it's love, because I feel love exists in them all. Sometimes, when I'm mad at her, I feel that it's just lust and temptation making me want her so badly, but whatever the feeling may be; it is most definitely real.

Sometimes I can't even control my emotions because of the confusion that I am feeling. I feel it is very unhealthy, so whenever this happens; I clear my mind to stop those feelings from taking over. I can't allow my temptations to control my actions, because that is not my description of being a man. I try to keep things going smooth and under control. I'll only allow my desires, temptations, lusts, and love to flow freely if everything is fine in our relationship.

Happiness is my true goal and something that I continuously strive for. It keeps me smiling and looking forward to a new day of even more happiness. What would we all do without it other than just be miserable?
Life is a blessing, not a mistake; so live it, love it, and try to always feel great!

Love and by: Anthony Dixon

The Coldest Winter

It was the coldest winter,
with below zero degree temperatures;
A disaster that made skin feel as if,
it was packed compact with splinters;
Just a walk out the door to the store,
was more than enough to injure;
Fore any soul in the cold,
was not that old mans' contender;
The wise wizard,
of blinding, blustering, blizzards;
and fierce winds blowing and throwing,
snowflakes into the faces of those not knowing;
Not nearly close to the places they're going,
growing weary with very little visibility;
because everywhere they look and go,
snow is all they see;
their souls exposed to the cold,
with nowhere to run, hide, or flee;
To get out of the path,
of Old Man Winters' wrath,
and escape his captivity!

3/25/05

All About: The Coldest Winter

The bitter cold Connecticut winter season of two-thousand and five made me vision one day of the coldest winter ever! A winter that made every other winter seem like summer! A bone-chilling, body numbing, nose running, snot freezing, teeth chattering, thought shattering winter!

I personified old man winter as the most ruthless, cold hearted, intimidating being alive as he came and wreaked havoc on the north! From now on; every winter you should properly dress for the occasion, because you'll never know what he could have in store! He could make the snow pour for hours more as he blows his wind that violently roars! Be careful how you speak of his name, because he could freeze your lips with freezing rain that would be frozen before it reached a drain, and caused many people to fall with broken bones' pain!

So be prepared when the leaves on trees start to fall from fright, as autumn pardons then cold wind enters! It quickly comes and goes, because it very well knows that it must get out of the sight of Mr. Old Man Winter; before he makes them quiver, and shiver from the Ice Aged impact that he delivers!

Love and by: Anthony Dixon

The Depths of My Soul

The depths of my soul exists
in this widely unsearched, vast,
and unknown universe that consists
of black holes, suns, moons,
stars, plasma, and gases.
In the center of the dark
where no one has ever entered these parts
that holds the key to my heart.
I am a deep soul!
In deep space!
Where the final frontier is never near,
because there is no ending to this place!

5/18/05

All About: The Depth of My Soul

To seek the depth of a persons' soul; you have to look beyond the surface, and see through to the spirit. The more the persons' spirit is free from bondage of any kind; the deeper their soul will be.

Tapping into the chi of individuality to the complexity of a person takes observance of their character. For examples: how they think; what they say; and how they act; are key ingredients in defining ones depth. How would you find your soul mate if you didn't pay attention to the depth of their soul? There; lies the naked truth of who they are, and what they are about. It is where you will find your likes and differences that will either make you an ideal couple, or give you the warning signs that tell you if you are headed for disaster.

Don't look for love blindly! Search with an open mind and heart; deeply for that special someone who's out there waiting for you. You are destined to find each other within the depths of your souls.

Love and by: Anthony Dixon

The Epiphany of Tiffany

T is for toweringly tall,
so that you will never fall or feel small.

I is for I apologize if I ever hurt you at all.

F is for friend that you can count on and call.

The other F is for fun
that I miss with you having a ball!

A is for at some time or another
everyone makes a mistake.

N is for no one is perfect.
Hearts do occasionally break!

& Y is for why can't we give it another try,
because you are the one & only apple of my eye!

9/6/05

The Good Fight (Jan.2006)

I won't quit, because I can't afford to give up the fight,
by any means necessary I have to make things right;
There is so much wrong that is going on,
but I know it is in Gods' sight;
and what he sees he doesn't like;
One of these days his almighty might will strike,
and I'm going to be on the good side;
fighting the good fight;

I have to keep on moving, showing, and proving;
I know if I put all my faith in him;
We'll be winning and not losing,
because I'm on his side!
I swallow any kind of pride,
because, from the all seeing and knowing
I can not hide!

I'm going to keep my head up high until I touch the sky,
surely that'll be the day I die,
or at least the part of me that's flesh,
but that's the day my spirit will rise!
and my soul will finally rest!
That'll be the day I take flight to higher heights
with angels' wings to sing for the Almighty
King of Kings;
giving the Lord his praise for his Amazing Grace;
because his blood was shed for the living,
but from the dead he was raised above all things!
Now I embrace his guiding light
that shines down on my face;
So day and night
I'm going to keep on fighting the good fight!

The Matter

It is not invisible! It is there! Solid as a rock!
Taking up space as wasted time is ticking on the clock!
Everyone can see it,
but still, to some it is a shock!
Finding it difficult to believe it,
but it is real; believe it or not!
Even though I may be down, wear a frown,
and wish all of this nonsense would stop!
I pray just before I lay down
to awaken back on the top!
Sometimes people find small acts of kindness
in the patters of their heart.
Then ask me, what is going on? What is wrong?
and what's the matter's, where it starts;
I wonder if they tossed themselves the same question
as they crossed along my path?
and thought with deep affection,
before they disturbed the little peace that I have!
Concerned of what's the matter with me
seemed to be what they wanted to learn!
But why me, when I am one!
when most of this world will surely burn!
Maybe they asked me a question of lame
to try to keep my hopes up high!
So that I may make a change
before the coming of the day I die,
when I pray that I am not summoned into the flames!
Tired of hearing the same words appearing!
Not fearing; I looked into their eyes!
and asked myself, what sense is in this question
in which I am so antagonized?

but I answered it back with sense and discretion,
and calmly replied!
The world is the matter!
The great pearl between heaven and hell!
who knows where we will go here-after?
no one has ever come back to tell the tale!
When there was no time to chit chatter,
and all else had failed!
When chaos' bullets scattered,
and left nothing but empty shells!
The situation we're facing is not a joke,
so it calls for absolutely no laughter!
That will only eventually, consequently
leave everyone choked;
In this hole of a world and huge area of disaster!
filled with pedophile, child molesting pastors!
Evil people hiding behind the churches steeple
like needles in haystacks in one huge pasture!
Seeking refuge after the guiding light shines
on their misguided work of lucifer!

Many will be found and some will drown
in the polluted sea trying to flee!
The wasteland that's supposed to stand
all for one and one for all,
but it doesn't stand for me!
I can see the rockets red glare,
and those bombs bursting in air!
Where- we are not united, but stand divided to fall!
In a place also called this country tis of thee!
but it tis not my country at all!
Now, it's a shame when political,
and religious corruption is to blame
for high jacked planes, and drug lords importing cocaine!
The truth hurts! It's inside work!

and the children are feeling the pain!
Mother Nature has a headache,
from people making mistakes!
and Father Time has no more time to wait!
so extinction is our fate!
So keep the world in mind!;-- Over matters! –
humankind throws over their shoulders!
doesn't care to look after, and leaves behind!
Making matters even worse!
because soon, there won't be any room for clean air
or water, and we will all die of suffocation and thirst;
depending on what happens first!
because the world is angered and we are endangered
by the violent shakes of the earth!
causing killer tsunamis to birth,
silently from the ocean floor!
telling no one what is in store
until those grave waves come crashing,
and screams abruptly short-stop laughing,
on what was once a happy shore that is no more!
or volcanoes blowing their tops
and raining bouldering fallen rocks,
that comes to a smoldering stop!
knocking down your door as lava continues to pour!
I can keep on going as problems are still growing!
but I rather stop! and start showing solutions to solving!
The matters at hand as I devise a plan.
If not knowing, I'll research the answers revolving.
and for those that don't know,
and in the future ask me what's the matter!
I will answer briefly,
because I don't won't to make anyone madder or sadder!
I will respond in the shortest of sentences,
stating matter is the subject of interest!
Circumstances, facts, or events, in surrounding conditions!

Trouble or physical substance,
or for something to be important!
That's exactly what the matter is,
to answer their pop quiz!
or I might just say keep on your way!
because it's none of your bleeping bizz!

1/11/04

All About: The Matter

The world was, and is always going to be full of problems; unless we all come together and find the solutions to solve them! So many things go wrong in this far from perfect world. Leaving many people wondering; what is the world coming to? Is an end that hard to figure out?! Ask of a Christians point of view, and they will speak that it is written in revelations. But first ask of yourself because there in each and every one of us lies the future of our nations. All of us together are the problems, and the solutions of the world. We must sort out all of the ones that are creating the problems, so that we may peacefully get rid of their pollution. We must search high, so their wastes will not flow low, so they won't infect and effect the ones that are trying to correct. We must take it step by step; until these problems are met with answers and solutions, so that no more secrets from us are being kept! The world is in our hands! We must make the right choices, organize and plan! Then demand action by lifting our voices! We must take things more seriously, and cut out some of our laughter; to pay more attention to, and clearly listen to exactly what's the matter!

Love and by: Anthony Dixon

The Messenger

Lord, tell me and I will tell all the world!
Polish my mind and it will shine with a glare
like a rare, black, and precious pearl;
Send me a sign,
and I will make it known that you sent it;
I'm just a messenger, who's repented
for all the sins I've committed;
I admit it! I did it!
This, that, and the third,
but while doing my time for the crime
I kept my eyes in line with his word!
They set me free as a bird,
allowing me to soar and think more about
better things to explore;
Revealing exactly what the purpose of my life is for!
I remember the time God noticed me
when he heard my plea for help;
I was confused and he focused me,
then guided me through the steps;
He told me to write poetry
and arm myself with pen and paper in hand
to be about his plan!
Then I will surely be great in this world,
I will clearly take a stand!
because I will be his messenger!

3/22/06

The Misery of History

The misery of history still haunts and taunts me;
so it is not a mystery
why Uncle Sam says that he wants me;
but he can no longer have me, because now I'm free;
although if this was the year fifteen-fifty-three;
Uncle Sam and his clan would surely hang me from a tree;
rape the women of my family,
while they burn crosses on my foreign lawn, and yell out profanity;
in vain in the name of Christianity;
What is this if not insanity?
When countless lives were slain from being tortured,
until their bodies were numbed from pain;
after they fought the hating discrimination,
by escaping the enslaving;
paving the roads to freedom
that would leave them distraught;
Dreading what would happen to them
if they were ever caught;
Breaking those shackles and chains,
to be hunted down like wild game;
High crimes, that in these times,
that would have quickly received the death penalty;
An action that would left only a small fraction
of the enemy;
So damn Uncle Sam, Cuz - he isn't even kin to me;
Although he pretends to be,
nor is he a friend of me;
because all he ever did was hinder me;
in one way or another, and neither my mother or father
ever spoke of having a brother - of another shade of color;
that for so long - represented the unjust prejudice,
Going on for so long,- that was so wrong;

making the African family weak,
trying to keep us from growing strong;
In a nation that had human beings bound to a plantation;
slaving in fields that yield plenty with stomachs nearly
empty;
and all they got was beaten and not one penny;
Shackled and chained, some passing out or dying from
strain;
from the strenuous, continuous, vigorous hardships,
that were not meant for them to gain;
because the intent was for the money to be spent,
for more English settlements that came across the sea in
ships,
from England and Spain;
Carrying my ancestors dignity-through misery-to histories'
shame.
This is far from a mystery,
It is the misery of history

10/12/04

All About: The Misery of History

I wrote this poem as I looked at the world, and thought about everything that I was seeing in the present and everything I had remembered seeing in the past. Being of African descent; which I am very proud of, I also feel a lot of pain going through the struggle of life. I can't help but reflect and pay respect to my African ancestors who made it possible for me to be here today, and experience the rights of freedom that I have! I think about the fact that if Abraham Lincoln didn't create the Emancipation Proclamation, and stood up for slaves; we might still be enslaved today! If someone after Abe would have done it instead of him; we would have been set back even more years, decades, or centuries; and probably going through now what Martin, Malcolm, The Black Panthers, their followers and the rest of our people went through back then! Poverty is an everyday part of my life and many others of my nationality, because when our ancestors were slaves; the caucasions were getting rich off of their labor. They killed and made the rest of the Native Americans migrate off of the land that they were born and raised on! It was the only place they knew to call home. The caucasions then took control of the land and established their colonies and plantations.

When my ancestors were finally freed from the physical bondage of slavery; they had nothing! They were promised forty acres and a mule; which was just another deceiving white lie! My ancestors were set free, but free to go where? They had nothing but the clothes on their back.

They had no land, no house, and they were stranded without a way to get back to their original homeland. I wasn't in slavery, but I definitely feel the effects of it! Most of us have to start from scratch; because most caucasions inherited the money, and land that their ancestors received from my ancestors slaving in the cotton fields and building this nation up from its evil foundation! The abuse that my people went through is tragic, and I can only think, vision, and imagine what it was like! At the same time that is all anyone would want to do, because thinking and visioning about it strikes more than enough fear and sorrow into ones heart without even having to be there! I thank God every day that I didn't experience that cruel moment in time, but many of my ancestors were not as fortunate; and my heart goes out to them! They will never be forgotten for going through the misery of history!

Love and by: Anthony Dixon

The Perfect Greeting

You greet me in the morning with your sunshine,
and hug me with its' rays;
You embrace me at night
with your moon, and starlight
These are reasons I give you Praise;
You gave your only Sons' life for me,
For his sake my soul could be saved;
You walk with me through my lifes' journey,
even when the roads are not paved;
You gave me life,
and the breath that I breathed on my first day;
You shined your light, and it dawned on me:
these words that you would say;
"You are a child of God, I love you,
and from me you shouldn't stray,
but if you do my lost sheep, I will find you
and with me you will always stay;
Always pray, and if someone asks of you;
Reply yea or nay;
Sacrifice for me and in life there won't be
any price that you can't pay;"
and from his perfect greeting
he was teaching me
how to be a man of God about my ways!

2006

The Reason Is Poetry

There is a reason for everything:
For the constant changes of the seasons,
from summer to spring;
The reason is poetry in motion,
flowing like the waves of the ocean;
while running through my veins,
healing my pain, and keeping me sane,
so I remain to gain;
With wisdom sharpening my vision,
making my precision
one-hundred percent straight aim;
Giving me the ability,
to reach for the stars with no holding bars
keeping me encaged, so I can release my rage;
through poetry;
It notices me;
It focuses me;
It frees my mind,
It shows me signs;
It's even in my chemistry;
As a matter of fact,
to be exact;
Poetry is beautifully me!

2004

The Second Coming

Lord cast down your lightening rod!
With sword, strike fast and release your wrath!
Clear the path of all evil doers
by giving this dirty world a bath!
Cleanse away all the bloodshed of men!
Singe their skin of sins with fire and brimstone,
Because many are liers!
They don't believe in you
as if they put themselves here on their own!
Non-believers, cons, and deceivers;
But on judgment day they all will probably say:
They wish they weren't such under achievers!
By refusing to give you praise, it only shortens their days
In life, they purposely go astray from the right way;
knowing they will all pay the price!
of hell if they fail God trials and ultimate test,
and there souls will scream and yell
where the devil dwells
when their bodies are laid to rest!

March 2006

The Storm

The night was calm and warm;
perfect weather conditions for a storm;
There wasn't even a breeze,
to do the leaves on the trees any harm;
As it started to rain the towns' alarm rang
a loud iron clang, and banged
in the peoples' eardrums to warn;
The quiet night suddenly turned into a riot of fright,
and frantic panic rushed rampant
through the town peoples' manic;
Fore they knew that not too far off into the distance
was destruction and damage;
Hysteria flooded the area as the rain fell down,
and pounded the ground even heavier
as breaking heartbeats raced with fate to escape
to make it quickly to the storm cellar;
Knowing all those would perish… if a second too late,
and would not live to tell the tale of the tellers!
From the inside of the door
they heard the sound of a rustling roar
that tore up everything in it's path;
It swept the dunes like brooms,
and still kept coming for more,
as the people embraced and waited;
Not knowing what was in store,
but felt the overwhelming wrath of its' mass,
through the rumbling floor;
They trembled, although closely assembled,
and under the dim lit candles they kindled;
Their mind states crashed into a mental wreck!
As they prayed the storm would pass,
without granting them a certain death;

So their nervousness could finally dwindle!
The wind hissed and howled so foul and brute,
as it picked up and ripped up trees
right out of the ground by their roots
that stranded and landed some even through roofs
with branches sticking out of the top of houses as proof!
All those who lived this tale will tell the truth
of the storm that came with little warning
when they were a youth!
When ten minutes seemed to last forever,
due to the very worst kind of weather,
that made all feel life was coming to an end;
Saved first, were children, women, then men
and when they finally came out of the cellar,
they found the wind had knocked down all their shelter;
but through it all, they still had each other!
If your home is gone, then you can rebuild another,
but you can not rebuild,
your family, friends, and significant others!

April 2005

The Young Tree

Still;
It bothers no one,
standing quiet as can be.
It lives through the coldest winter chills,
incapable for you and me.
It's life was granted when its' seed was planted
by nature or humanity,
to sow the earth and be given birth
to a growing breed of trees.

The rain and sunshine feeds its' hunger;
providing everything it needs.
The rain is absorbed by the roots down under,
and the sunshine sprouts healthy newborn leaves;
It will continue to grow for possibly centuries;
as long as natures' nourishment flows;
if it is not hacked by the axe of a lumberjack,
because even the trees have enemies!
If they could walk and talk,
My God, would they have a story to tell!
I only can dream of seeing them in action,
but what would happen by chance if one of them fell!
Came down crashing to the ground, smashing!
It's branches thrashing,
and crushing everything under it like shells!
I wonder how long will it take for him to get up,
without the assistance of a lady tree
with a whole lot of junk in her trunk!
because they don't have knees,
So they would have to lift each other back up.

They could tell me my history of the sorrowful ways
my ancestors were mistreated,
and hung as slaves in earlier days;
I'd find out all about their sacred jungles;
before man had devised a plan,
to make most of their rain forests crumble!
They provide us with oxygen,
so without them, what would we do?
Other than perish from suffocation;
and die colors of black and blue!
I really do appreciate all of you trees
for being there for me;
You are the keys to our survival,
because without you, we couldn't be!

So I will take this time to say thank you Pine,
and every other family of trees;
I love you all!
Keep growing tall, and chilling in the breeze.

4/21/05

Thinking of You

I think of you when I am weak,
and also when I am strong;
Twelve hours in the day time,
and twelve all night long;
My spirit is lifted in your very presence,
because your essence is of a queen,
that flows through your bloodstream;
At sight you give off fluorescent,
beams of bright light;
That by any means,
gets me through my worst dreams,
and darkest nights;
I hold on to our memories like Socrates,
held on to his philosophies;
as I jot down notes of your joy
to add them to my own collection,
as a reflection of Heavens' properties;
Thinking possibly one day,
I might get down on my bended knee;
to put a ring on your finger,
and ask you to marry me;

Having visions of
the releasing of two white doves,
as a signature of our love;
Birds of the same feather,
together forever, flying up above;
Its' value is very sentimental,
and essential that it goes on,
like occasional run- on's sentences in my memo;
There is no need for apostrophes,
for something so satisfying and simple;
As we make reservations for self preservation;
By meditating the mental and educating our temple;
All the time knowing,
I can not stop in the name of love,
because our love keeps going;
Growing like the knowledge tree into infinity,
Crossing all boundaries that once seemed to be;
Parted like the Red Sea
when enemies refused to let Gods' people free;
Blowing like passionate kisses in the wind,
that last for eternity;
Making love to my skin through your serenity,
I will forever be, thinking of you.

2004

All About: Thinking of You

One of my famous ex's was the inspiration behind this poem. It wasn't a second in a day, that went by; that I didn't think of her. Everything that I did; I felt I did it for us, but for some reason there was always a lack of trust. I found out the reason; a year and a lot of money spent on her later; that she was a no good, gold digging, should be Oscar

Award winning actress, playing the role of a loving and caring young lady. After I found this out; I could have played the role of Jason, or Micheal Myers, but horror was never my thing. Only love, drama, comedy, and action roles played by the perfect gentleman were up my alley. It took me a long time to replace those thoughts of her with fresh memories, but I admit that they weren't as memorable. Maybe I should keep my mind occupied on something instead of someone, so I wouldn't have to make such of a drastic turn in my life if something went wrong.

Love and by: Anthony Dixon

To An Expecting Mother

To an expecting mother,

an exceptional lover,

of all her children to bare;

She's a professional teacher,

a promising youth outreacher,

and provides them with nurturing care;

I wish you and your children,

the best of health and prosperities wealth;

In the new life that you all will share.

5/11/05

All About: To An Expecting Mother

I was typing in a computer lab one day when an expecting mother came in and sat at the computer beside me. She was very attractive, and I could easily understand the reasons of why she was pregnant.
Who wouldn't want a beautiful woman as the mother of their children?

I chatted with her briefly; telling her congratulations, and mentioned that I wrote poetry. As I spoke to her, the title of this poem came to mind, and I later wrote down the words to it. It pays tribute to all the mothers that gave birth when they had an option not to. If it wasn't for my mother deciding to have her first child even though she was very young at the age of sixteen; I wouldn't even be here! I am very thankful, and more than grateful to experience this blessing of life! It is one of a kind and I appreciate it dearly. Out of all living things that I could have been born, I was born a human being in one of the greatest time periods of mankind!

I give my thanks and respects to all of you mothers for sharing the gift of life, and passing it down to be carried on through your children. May God be with your generations of the future!

Love and by: Anthony Dixon

$Value% Or Values

If money and materials

were ever an issue between us;

Then I would not need this tissue

to wipe the tears from my eyes,

because I love you and miss you!

Jan. 2005

All About: $Value% or Values

I wrote this poem to signify the difference between value and values; because some people get them confused, and falsely accuse others of being about one; when they are actually about the other. Money can't buy my love. It may buy temporary pleasure, but love is a priceless treasure. It is full of real morals and values of integrity, and not the negativity that comes with materials and money. Some people connect with others for the wrong reasons. To know the difference you have to know yourself, your standards, and know what hints from the gold diggers' traits to look out for. Love is not blind if you open your mind and eyes to see it.

Love and by: Anthony Dixon

Vengeance

Relentless it asks for no repentance!
It fears nothing!
Not even the toughest jail sentence!
Not even death!
It could care less for its' breath,
and once started it doesn't stop until it's finished
when there are no painful memories left!
Then just when you thought this force
you fought was diminished!
It came back to attack
to take care of its' unfinished business!
Knocking on the door waiting for you to say,
who is it?
Not knowing, the unexpected came to pay you a visit!
If it knows it will not live long enough
to accomplish what it intended!
It will pass those painful memories down
to be found in its' apprentice,
and as long as they are still in existence
it will show persistence, and tolerate no resistance!
It will make sure those memories will not replenish,
and until this is done its' mission is endless!
What I'm talking about, is stalking about!
It is better known as vengeance!

3/9/05

Voice The Choice

Uplifted, I voice the choice,
to be heard in my own words;
To rejoice aloud and proud,
and float on the clouds of tomorrows' day
without sorrow and say;
I made that choice!
The choice to show and prove
to make as many moves as I choose,
and be happy or sing the blues!
To feel free to be
anywhere in the world that I want to be!
To see what I want to see!
Free to flee society to be alone in privacy
to soak in my bitter sweet memories,
and make choices of infinite possibilities!
My freedom of choice and uplifted voice
will supply the power I need indeed
to march on over the problems
that no one's solving triumphantly!
Leaving the only taste of victory they get
coming from the bottom of my feet
as I righteously step!

2004

All About: Voice the Choice

The freedom of choice and the right to voice your opinion is a very powerful privilege! Many people still don't use those privileges wisely, and some don't use them at all! We all have to stand up for our rights instead of letting people take advantage of them! There is a message to be given, and you must give it!

Only you can stand for you! I like to make my own decisions, and do what I feel! I don't need anyone else dictating my actions or words! I am free! Free to do, and free to be myself! Rules and regulations are everywhere you go, but no matter what; I'm free and use my creative mind to the fullest!

Voice the choice for your words to be heard!
Act now by speaking up for what you believe in!

Love and by: Anthony Dixon

Walking Through the Darkness

(All About Survival)

I'm walking through the darkness,
and hoping to find light!
Using my inner senses sharpness,
by seeing with only my insight!
Being careful of every step that I take,
because I can not afford to fall!
I'm not able to see the ground beneath me
from being surrounded by darkness's walls!
I am not aware of my surroundings
whether I look left or right,
so I try to slow down my hearts pounding
from being blinded in the night!
As fog falls upon me
so does the feeling of slight fright,
but I put all my fears aside
confident everything would be alright!

I kept on moving forward towards my only goal!
In search of a light shining bright
to guide my wandering soul,
and to help me get through the darkness of the night!

I stumbled deeper into darkness's jungle
remaining humble and quiet
as if someone had hushed and hid
from the bum rush of a riot!
Keeping my poise as I walked
the only noise that was heard
was from brush being crushed
along with the snapping of twigs!
Then mentally a light shined when an idea came to mind!
of how to get out of this darkness before I ran out of time!
Without doubting the capabilities of what I could achieve;
although I have never been boy scouting
I kneeled down on my knees!
To the ground, felt around, and gathered some dry leaves!
I believe I sorted them out from at least a thousand
that had fallen off the trees!
I then felt and picked up two large sticks,
and began rubbing them together.
For what seemed to me more like forever!
Lucky me!
I was fortunate fore it had been fairly dry weather!
Then all of a sudden
the start of sparks came from my rubbing!
The heat of friction became a flame
that was slowly erupting!
A small fiery glow that seemed almost tame
barely large enough to show,
and at that moment I just hoped that the wind didn't blow,
it didn't snow, nor rain!

I quickly reached into my pocket with stealth and aim
to pull out some pieces of paper
on which I had written some names!
I stuck them in the fire,
and watched as it quickly rose higher!
Then I searched all of my pockets;
my papers' supplier.
Good thing I'm a writer, and also a fighter!
I'm also a tobacco smoker,
but somewhere in the darkness I lost my lighter!
Now finally, I can see exactly where I'm at!
No longer am I directly in darkness,
but my surroundings are black!
With ease I lit the dry leaves,
then gathered dry limbs and branches
so the fire could feed!
I was careful not to smother it!
I made sure it could breathe!
I fathered it and nature mothered it
taking caring of its' needs!
The fire warmed and alarmed me
of the next things for me to do!
So I started making torches to help guide my way through!
I was tired and weak,
and thought how would I feed my hunger?
So I searched not too far from my campfire
for wild fruits and berries of the summer.
Once found; I returned to my camp
guided by the torch I held high as my noble lamp!

From some of the fruits and berries that I crushed up;
I drank down their juices in my new bamboo cup,
but what I really wanted was cooked meat to eat!
Let me think!
If I capture two rabbits

I can use their hide as shoes for my feet!
If I kill a deer I can use his skin for a blanket or sheet!
Then cook them over my fire,
and fall into a good nights sleep!
So I looked for limber timber strong enough for a bow!
Then I remembered strong, stringy vines!
I know just where they grow!
What I'll do is choose thinner bamboos
so my arrows can cruise;
like a sparrow zooming in on my target
before it has the chance to move!
After I've assembled my weaponry and its' utensils;
I will start my hunt!
Hoping to hear the sound of a wild boars' grunt,
or any beast that moves in front
of my sharpened spear that is far from blunt!

3/7/05

Weeping Willow

As my eyes water and cry,
and soft tears soak my cloaked pillow;
My head hangs low as the limbs,
of the weeping willow outside of my bedroom window;
Its' branches swing and hang beautifully lame;
from which came its' name;
Appearing almost ashamed;
just the way nature arranged;
Then a wind blew mellow;
and plucked its' stringed vines like a cello;
Until leaves started to rain of green and yellow,
that flew and blew unto my window pain;
The tree limbs danced in the wind

as the brisk breeze freed the leaves
that summersaulted and spinned;
In flight like a kite as their ride neared an end,
but they got caught and was given another lift
by a swift drift of wind, and then their ride began again;
They tossed, turned, and flipped;
rose, nose dived, and dipped
on what would be their final trip;
Each leaf, a captain going down with its' ship;
gliding and riding on the last waves to the grave
paraded by the wind to its' final resting place;
It was a ceremony beyond beautiful;
It was also poetical and musical,
as each one landed on its' last note;
In a stream that gleamed beams of current by the sun,
as it quietly took them afloat!

2/16/05

What Is Your Name?
(Heaven or the Closest Thing To It)

I sat and patiently pondered at
your delighting sighting
until my brainstorms thundered,
and plundered lightning;
I wondered until I came to two conclusions,
Either one: I am in heaven,
or two: I am under;
Though your beauty made choosing
somewhat confusing;
but if this is heaven,
then you are truly a blessing
that I will never forget;

This is my honest confession,
though nervous and starting to sweat;
and if this isn't heaven,
then it must be the closest to it
that I will ever get;

I can't resist!
Excuse me miss,
I don't believe we have met;
My name is Anthony Dixon,
What's yours?
Anxious to hear her tell as she held me captive
under one of her attractive love spells;
then smiled and replied, " Rashelle";
Instantly triggering mental pictures,
of charming wedding bells;
With her as my bride;
kissing after lifting her veil;
Then being greeted outside
by brown rice showering
from the throwers' wedding pails;
So I must be in heaven,
because this just can't be hell;
Because devils don't groove too cool with
beautiful songs of acoustic music,
and soulfully shake their tails;
But Rashelle,
if I'm wrong and this really isn't heaven,
then the blessing of your presence
must be the closest thing to it.

4/2/05

All About: What is Your Name?
(Heaven or the Closest Thing To It)

I wrote this poem inspired by a beautiful young lady by the name of Rashele. I admire such of a lovely lady, and decided to write a poem about her. I knew little of her except for her name, but her beauty told a story of its' own; that I could capture in a poem. I looked at her and thought, until I had the perfect vision of words organized to describe what I'd seen.

I enjoyed writing this poem wishing that every bit of it was true when it came to myself being in it. I was actually writing how I felt in the poem about her from just knowing her physical being from an occasional group session. It was more than my pleasure to write a poem for such of a beautiful sight to behold; that was actually a pleasure to my own sight. I told her later that evening what I was doing and told her that I'd let her read it as soon as I finished. I kept my word of course and she liked the poem, but I was also trying to win her heart and soul to be with me. It was worth a try, even though I didn't succeed. I guess she didn't qualify me as being in her league, but I at least felt a little closer to heaven from being in her presence.

Love and by: Anthony Dixon

Why Give Up?

Why give up?
When I have nothing to give up,
but my life in which I must live up!
Why surrender and accept defeat?
When it is my only life
that I would forfeit and cheat!
Why retreat? When there's a chance
the odds can be beat!
Why starve myself ?
When there is food to eat!
Why lay to rest in peace?
When I can lay and sleep!
Why blow my own horn?
When someone else can beep!
Why not count my blessings?
When I have counted sheep!
Why follow anyone?
When I am one unique!
Why sit down?
When I can sit up!
If I'm going too fast in speed;
Why slow down?
When I can slow up,
and last but not least;
why not take something down,
rather than give up!

4/1/05

All About: Why Give Up?

I wrote this poem dealing with the pressures of not knowing what the future held for me, and feeling that I had failed myself by not achieving my childhood goals. I was feeling the guilt after blaming myself for my own downfall, because the people who I wanted to point my fingers at; were nowhere around. I wasn't even sure if I wanted to know what the future held; or if I even wanted a future after feeling the pain of my past coming back to haunt me with the reality of my childhood goals and dreams being robbed by my own foolish ways and rebellious actions. I came to the conclusion, that I have come too far to give up! Give up for what? I asked myself. To only feel like a complete loser and failure? No! I will not except that! I know that I am better than that! These thoughts provoked me to write them down, and when I was finished, I titled it; Why Give Up? It is my struggle to persevere and still reach my expectations of happiness, despite my mistakes and losses from my past. It is encouragement to get me through the storm when all else seems to fail. It is my hope, dreams, and motivation; to guide me through the darkness.
Why give up? When there isn't a good enough reason to!

Love and by: Anthony Dixon

Wings of Freedom

I have wings,- not like a bird,
but wings that allow me to fly through spoken words!
Traveling at the speed of a javelin and
thrown like the spear of an African Mandingo Warrior;
Superior as the Zulu leaving you who
thinks I am inferior, similar to the interior walls
of a shelter showers' stall!
Filthy rich with disgust, must, and old mold,
beyond your control!
It's almost too hard to believe the disease it breeds
as it feeds upon the depressed human flesh
that hasn't had any rest in countless days and nights;
from wandering astray in the streets!
So please, close your eyes and open your mind
to find yourself free,- you lost black sheep!
We should be trying to reach each other
to teach each other,- my sisters and brothers!
Are we not the keepers of each other?
For those that have let ignorance consume their souls,
and in the process of consumption
caused them to malfunction;
leaving them nothing more than a hollow hole
where waste goes and is disposed of
when it's themselves who they should be ashamed of!
Damn near thirty and still wants to be a thug;
So quick to pick up a drug,
but slow to pick up responsibility,
because they want to get drunk as can be!
So they rather go to the liquor store and buy a 40;
Even though it's (4) for (0's) zeros
They want to impress that shorty with the drinks

to make her think their super ghetto fabulous heros;
Little do they know, those forty ounces- counted
only adds up to bad breath,
and somebody probably making a fool out of theirself!
So free yourself from the bondage of drugs and booze,
because if abused; it could be your liver,
or life that you lose;
You see, I write to help fight the good fight,
to enlightened those confused,
and to find the lost so they won't have to pay the cost;
and I use my word tools to reach them;
Hoping they will take flight like myself
on the spreaded Wings of Freedom!

10/26/04

All About: Wings of Freedom

I wrote this poem when I was staying in an emergency shelter and feeling physically tied up, and feeling the need to be more mentally free. So, I flew the coop on the wings of my words that night as I wrote Wings of Freedom. I reflected on the problems that I faced in the shelter, being homeless, and the problems that surrounded me everyday. To me, it is senseless that people are without food, and homes when this country is so wealthy. They give out cash prizes of thousands and millions of dollars every day, that could end homelessness if the money was given to that cause. It is just wrong. I sometimes escape from the hostage situation of society by flapping my wings of freedom and flying to a distant, isolated place; to gather my thoughts and feelings so I can remain strong in my situation. Come and fly with me!

Love and by: Anthony Dixon

With God In Mind

With God in mind,
you can stand the tests of time!
With God in mind,
there's not a feat that you can't climb!
He will show you the signs,
and everything will be just fine!
Just as long as you keep…
God in mind!

3/18/06

About the Author

From NC to CT,
Anthony Shaun (The Poetic Don) Dixon is proving he's the truth when it comes to poetry! He made his debut in the Poetic Rendezvous last summer of '05 at the New Haven Public Library, landing him in
the Inner City Newspaper. He then went on to be the feature poet of the month at Yale Barnes and Noble in August of '05, and now he's back with his versatile style of writing in his first book

"Poetical Praise, Passion, and Politicking."

-Every prized bookshelf should have one!-

Thank you all for supporting his positive vision
and God Bless!

Anthony Dixon

Made in the USA
Middletown, DE
27 May 2023

30808267R00116